EXPLORE LONDON'S SQUARE MILE

EXPLORE
LONDON'S
SQUARE MILE

2,000 Years of Heritage from the Romans to World Financial Centre

Lucy McMurdo

NEW
HOLLAND

Dedication

To Mac

Acknowledgements

The author would like would like to thank New Holland Publishers for commissioning this book, with particular thanks to Alan Whiticker, James Mills-Hicks, and Andrew Davies for their hard work and support.
I am also most grateful to Mick Bagnall, Andrew Buckingham and Nick Bodger and his team at the City of London Corporation for their valuable assistance.
My greatest thanks go to my husband, Mac, always so supportive, and whose wonderful photographs and maps fill the book.

Beefeaters

CONTENTS

View of the City from the South Bank – St Paul's and the Millennium Bridge

INTRODUCTION

This is a guidebook unlike most others written about London, as it is entirely devoted to the **Square Mile**, or as it also referred to, the **City of London**. Despite being the oldest part of the capital – with 2,000 years of colourful history – and the seat of many of London's and the country's great institutions, it is still relatively undiscovered by local and overseas visitors. This book aims to introduce you to some of the amazing things the City has to offer and covers its existence since Roman times as a major trading post, port and city right up to present-day as one of the world's great financial centres.

Despite a tiny population of around 8,000 the Square Mile generates an enormous amount of wealth for London and the United Kingdom, with more than 400,000 people coming to work here on a daily basis. This has led to an area that offers superb facilities: great restaurants, sky-high cocktail bars, fine-dining venues, clubs, hotels, ancient pubs and taverns, museums, attractions and an array of hidden gardens and open spaces in which to take time out. This is where London began – Roman **Londinium** – and you can still visit parts of the Roman wall, see remains of the amphitheatre, fort and bathhouse and view some of the amazing discoveries from the 1st to 5th centuries that are displayed within the Museum of London.

The City of London has the added advantage of not being overcrowded with tourists. It is really compact, so that you can walk from one side to the other easily in under 30 minutes and has so many themes: the Romans, devastation by fire (especially in the 1st, 17th and 20th centuries), the Lord Mayor and the City of London Corporation, livery companies, City churches, rivers (Thames, Fleet and Walbrook), legal London, the newspaper industry as well as its many American associations. The list is endless. Many films and television series are set here and make this area all the more recognisable. The architecture is stunning; ancient buildings stand cheek-by-jowl with modern towers and the skyline is forever

Inside The Old Bank of England

changing. New buildings are constantly proposed and the number of cranes in the City at any one time is simply exceptional.

Explore London's Square Mile takes the visitor on a tour around the area's wonderful intricate streets and alleyways. You will come across names of streets that describe by resident, product or trade what once took place here. Walk along Cornhill, Houndsditch, Old Jewry, Lombard Street, Milk Street, Fish Street Hill and Threadneedle Street to gain an idea of the diversity of the ancient City.

Interestingly, the Tower of London and Tower Bridge sit just outside the City boundary. As both are such landmarks and so connected with the Square Mile and the history of London, it is only fitting that they should be covered in this book. Likewise, information is included about some of the wonderful entertainment

The Duke of Wellington at Bank Junction

venues, shopping and markets that are on the City periphery, as they are really just an extension of the geographical Square Mile and patronised by those working and living in the City.

Through walks and text, the book sets out to show what makes the City tick: the type of companies based here, its enormous variety of financial and insurance institutions, its arts venues, activities and pageantry, and how the area is a buzzing 21st-century district, constantly evolving and moving forward.

This is the ideal book for anyone who wants to unravel the many different layers of the Square Mile. The City is not simply a place to work in, but an area rich in art, history, tradition and state-of-the-art architecture and there is always something new to see and to explore. It might be the smallest of London's 33 local authorities but is undoubtedly the richest and most significant.

HOW TO USE THE BOOK

All the chapters (except 1, 8 and 11) are laid out as a walk, beginning and ending at or near an underground (tube) station. Directions from one stop on the walk to another are given in *italics* throughout the text. To help you familiarise yourself with Roman London and the geography of the Square Mile, refer to the maps in the inside front and back covers. The map in the front of the book shows the present city, while the map at the back shows the outline of Roman London laid over the present city. The boundary of the Square Mile is shown with a purple broken line and the Roman city is outlined in yellow.

Most chapters open with a map showing major features or landmarks of the area and the numbers in circles on the map correspond to the numbers in bold square brackets (for example, [**8**]) found throughout the text. Due to the nature of the Square Mile, places, people and institutions are sometimes repeated in several different chapters. When this occurs, a red asterisk * alongside a chapter number will show where further information can be found (for example, *Chapter 10).

For detailed information about London's transport, refer to the **Travel in London** section at the end of the book. Crossrail, the United Kingdom's major transport engineering project taking place across central London, should be completed in the near future but until the project finishes, expect changes to the Underground and Overground timetables, especially on weekends. Transport for London's website (www.tfl.gov.uk) will give you up-to-the-minute information about any closures or engineering work due to take place.

When it opens, Crossrail will be renamed the **Elizabeth line** in honour of Queen Elizabeth II, and will provide fast links across the capital from Reading and Heathrow in the west to Abbey Wood and Shenfield in the east.

A glance at Transport for London's map illustrates how well the City is already served by the underground. It is also home to **four mainline railway termini** at Liverpool Street, Cannon Street, Moorgate and Fenchurch Street largely serving the commuter areas to the east, north and south-east.

My motivation in writing **Explore London's Square Mile** stems from my own very great pleasure in wandering about this spectacularly historic and yet so modern district. It is astonishing what you might find when you turn a corner – a Wren church, remains of the Roman wall, a modern sculpture, a 300-year-old pub, a lunch market or a garden in the sky … the list is endless! However you decide to spend your time in this wonderful compact and historic centre, make sure to turn off the main streets into the many alleyways and hidden labyrinthine passages. Here you are sure to discover the charm of the Square Mile and what makes it such an enticing and exciting place to visit.

The City has an exceedingly long and fascinating history and is full of traditions and pageantry. Readers who seek to discover more about its day-to-day workings should refer to some of the excellent guides written about it, such as *The City of London Directory & Livery Companies Guide*, *The City of London White Book* or *The City of London Freeman's Guide*.

St Paul's

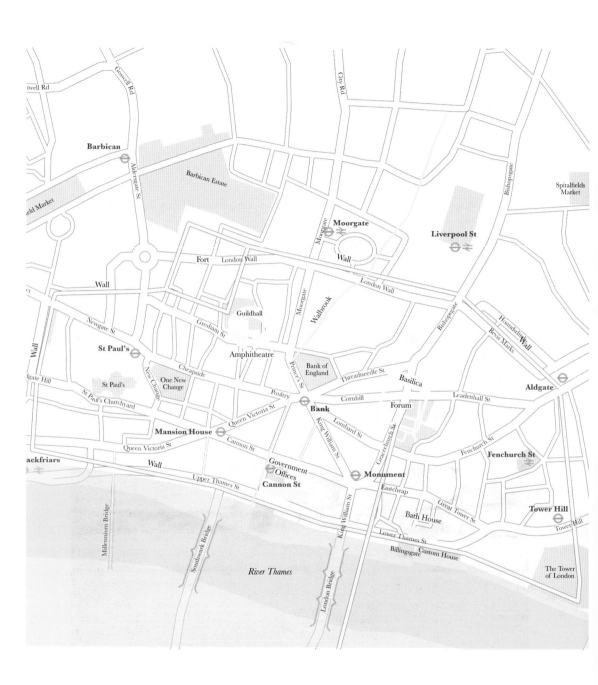

CHAPTER 1

SETTING THE SCENE

ORIGINS OF THE SQUARE MILE AND IMPORTANCE OF THE RIVER THAMES

It would be very easy to simply write a detailed account of the City of London's 2,000-year history but that is not the purpose of this book, and besides, there are many texts written on the subject already. For this reason, much of the City's history and its customs are incorporated into the appropriate chapters where the information is most relevant. This opening chapter looks at the beginnings of the Square Mile, showing its origins as a place of trade and commerce and how it developed its own unique form of government. It also describes how London's rivers have contributed to its status and prosperity and their role in City life today.

Night scene of the Square Mile

ROMAN LONDON

No introduction to the City of London can ignore the impact made by the Roman invasion in the early part of the 1st century ad. Before this time, London would have been little more than a settlement and certainly not the major centre it was to become as the northern outpost of the Roman Empire. Roman development of **Londinium**, as it was known, led to its great success as a trading hub. The Romans built the first timber bridge across the Thames and provided a range of amenities: public institutions such as a basilica (city hall) and forum (marketplace), as well as an amphitheatre, public baths, temples, government offices, housing, a city wall and fort.

The Romans recognised the significance of the River Thames and developed seaborne trade with Britain's European neighbours. The Thames estuary faced the mouths of three major rivers – the Rhine, Elbe and Scheldt – giving direct access to both the Roman Empire and overseas trade. Although during the Roman period the Thames was both wider and shallower than it is now, the stretch of water going east from London Bridge – the **Pool of London** – was deep enough to accommodate large ships. We know from excavations that the Romans faced the waterside banks with timber and constructed quays and landing places for boats to load and unload goods. There is evidence too of former wharves and warehouses dotted along the banks of the river.

Just inland, beneath and around the area of today's Leadenhall Market, were once the majestic law courts, main administrative centre and marketplace – the very heart of Londinium. Twentieth century archaeological investigation has also unearthed a Temple of Mithras, a 2nd-century fort, a bathhouse, public baths and remains of a vast amphitheatre (situated beneath Guildhall Yard) that would have seated as many as 7,000 people.

As most of Londinium's remains still lie 7 m (23 ft) below ground, archaeological investigations by **Museum of London Archaeology** (MOLA) generally take place before foundation work commences on any new development within the City's

Part of the Roman wall

boundaries. Some wonderful objects have surfaced over the years on account of MOLA's work; perhaps the most recent examples are the Bloomberg tablets, uncovered remarkably well-preserved in the wet mud of the Walbrook valley beneath Bloomberg Place. Today, many of MOLA's finds are on display within the Museum of London (www.museumoflondon.org.uk) and they are a truly incredible record of everyday domestic and commercial life in Londinium. Here you will find articles such as metalwork, jewellery, clothing, shoes, combs, hairpins, industrial tools, coins, glass, leather, bones and pots, as well as Roman pavements and mosaics. A marvellous example of the latter, the Bucklersbury Pavement is an almost intact floor mosaic that dates from AD250. Discovered in 1869 in the area between Poultry and Queen Victoria Street, it was considered such a great wonder that it attracted a crowd of more than 50,000 people who willingly queued for hours just to catch a glimpse of it.

The Roman way of life has left its mark on the City of London above ground too. The Roman road network still exists today and several impressive sections of its city wall have survived (particularly near the Barbican and at Tower Hill). A glance at some of the City's buildings (for example, Mansion House and the Royal Exchange), built with grand facades, columns and pediments – is also proof of the enduring influence of Roman architecture in the Square Mile.

Trajan

FROM ROMAN TO NORMAN INVASION

After the Roman departure from Londinium in the 5th century, much of the city was abandoned. Londoners moved west to **Lundenwic**, the area around present-day Covent Garden and Aldwych, until an upsurge in Viking raids during the 9th century forced them to return to the protection of the walled city.

By the reign of Edward the Confessor (1042–66), the City of London was once again an important trading centre, wealthy and with a sizeable population. As such it was able to command certain freedoms and gained rights from the Crown to run its own affairs in return for supporting and loaning the king money to fund his domestic and overseas policies. At this time, the City of London was governed by 'elder' men (Aldermen), who convened at the Court of Husting, the supreme court of the City. Their work was both administrative and judicial. By the late 12th century, the role of Mayor was established and the City's citizens were granted the right by King John, in a charter of 1215, to elect a Mayor annually. In time, the Aldermen called upon 'wise and discreet' citizens to attend their meetings and before long the group was meeting regularly and became known as the Common Council. It is from the City's ancient democratic system of governance of the Courts of Aldermen and Common Council that Britain's local and national parliamentary governmental system is largely based.

In 1066 following the death of Edward the Confessor, William of Normandy defeated Harold at the Battle of Hastings and then marched towards London besieging the city for many weeks. The citizens bravely withstood his attack until eventually the Aldermen conceded to William's rule in exchange for recognition of their urban liberties. The document drawn up to confirm this agreement became known as the **'William Charter – London Charter of Liberties'**. It was the first law that the new king made after his coronation, only four and a half lines long, yet of the utmost significance; it provided for the preservation of ancient liberties to the citizens of London, ceding to them Crown prerogatives such as privileges, liberties, protections and franchises. Never before had the monarch yielded such liberties to a group of citizens and it opened the way for people living in other cities to make similar requests for such freedoms. It is claimed that the William Charter actually laid down the foundation of Britain's parliamentary democracy, a model later spread by Britain throughout the world. In 1215 – almost 150 years later – Article IX of the Magna Carta signed by King John once again confirmed the earlier charter, ensuring the preservation of London's ancient liberties.

Both the William Charter and Magna Carta are on display in London: the former is exhibited in the City of London Heritage Gallery (beside Guildhall), while the latter is lodged in the British Library on Euston Road, close to St Pancras station.

THE RIVER THAMES
AND THE CITY RIVERSIDE

The tidal River Thames has always played a major role in London's history, as it connects the British Isles with the European continent and trade routes. For many centuries it was the main artery of the city, filled with vessels transporting cargo and ferrying citizens along the river.

In addition to the River Thames, Roman Londonium was served by the **Fleet** and **Walbrook** rivers. These waterways have since been largely channelled in sewers below ground but they were both highly important in their day, and it is still possible to see their course in the geography of the City as you walk round its streets.

The River Fleet still begins its course in the heights of Hampstead Heath, about 10.5 km (6½ miles) north-west of the City, and flows into the Thames by Blackfriars Bridge. There is little indication now of its former significance but it was once a major river with its own estuary and tidal mill, with thriving industry along

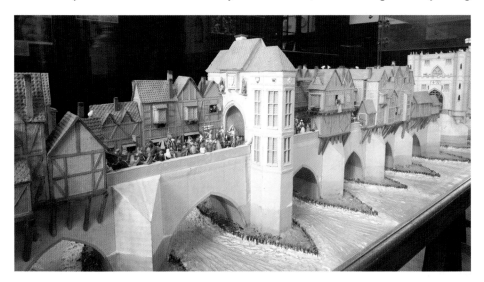

Model of the medieval London Bridge

its banks. In contrast, the course of the Walbrook was less than 3.2 km (2 miles) long, flowing from the eastern edge of the City amid the City's two hills at Cornhill and Ludgate. Situated right at the very core of Londinium, it was where much of the industry and trading took place. It is interesting to note that, 2,000 years on, the Walbrook valley is still very much an area for commerce, though nowadays revolving around business and finance rather than industries such as glass, pottery and the leather trades.

For hundreds of years, the banks of the Thames were a hive of industry; there were wharves, quays, warehouses as well as shipbuilding yards. Remnants of these have been discovered in recent archaeological digs in the Square Mile, providing us with proof of the area's rich heritage as a commercial centre.

Up until the mid-18th century, **London Bridge** was the only crossing over the Thames in central London. The medieval stone bridge built by Peter de Colechurch between 1176 and 1209 consisted of 19 narrow, uneven arches and was lined with buildings: shops, houses (up to seven storeys high), a chapel, a palace, a drawbridge, gatehouses, communal latrines and even waterwheels. An excellent model of it can be seen within St Magnus the Martyr church on Lower Thames Street (just east of the present-day London Bridge). The bridge's slender arches together with its broad pier bases had a significant impact on the water flow, so that there were some winters (particularly between the 17th and early 19th centuries) when the river upstream of the bridge became impassable as the water froze over. Despite the inconvenience, Londoners took full advantage of the situation, holding frost fairs on the iced-over Thames. Shops, booths and market stalls would appear (like pop-ups today!); there would be horse-and-coach races, bull baiting, shows and skating and it was a time of great revelry.

After 600 years, it became clear that the bridge had outlived its usefulness and a new five-arch stone bridge was built to replace it in 1831. Designed by Scottish civil engineer John Rennie, its structure allowed the tide to flow more freely and

London Bridge model in St Magnus the Martyr church

this, together with the later 19th-century embankment of the Thames, meant that freezing of the river became less common and eventually ceased.

During Queen Victoria's reign (1837–1901), several new bridges were constructed as London's trade and its dominant position in the British Empire grew. By the end of the 19th century, new crossings had been built at Blackfriars (road and railway bridges), a railway bridge at Cannon Street station and in 1894, the iconic Tower Bridge was completed. Throughout the 1800s and early 1900s, off-river docks were constructed to help ease congestion along the river but even then it was teeming with vessels. The Upper Pool, particularly between the Tower of London and London Bridge, was packed with ships awaiting inspection and assessment at Customs House and the river was buzzing with activity. This all came to an end by the 1960s, when new methods such as containerisation and the development of coastal deepwater ports challenged earlier practices.

London's docks died almost overnight and the port's activities ceased giving rise to regeneration of the dockland areas and the development of the Canary Wharf financial district. Today, the Pool of London sees a steady flow of river traffic but the boats are more likely to be ferrying tourists up and down the river rather than bringing in food and produce from around the globe. Port activities have moved away from the City, downstream to Tilbury freeing up the Thames for leisure activities. Former warehouses and industrial buildings have been transformed into highly desirable housing and many have fabulous views of Tower Bridge and the Tower of London.

Interestingly, neither of these icons is actually located within the Square Mile. Tower Bridge is owned and managed by Bridge House Estates, a charitable trust set up in the 13th century to maintain London Bridge, and is overseen by a committee of the City of London Corporation. Despite appearing to be quite ancient, the bridge is little more than 120 years old, only opening in 1894 and specifically designed in the Gothic style to complement the style of its neighbour, the Tower of London.

TOWER BRIDGE

Designed by City Architect Sir Horace Jones (also responsible for Leadenhall, Billingsgate and Smithfield Markets), the bridge is probably one of London's most recognisable landmarks. Visitors from far and wide stop to watch as its two great bascules open and shipping passes through on its way along the Thames. (You will find details of opening times online at www.towerbridge.org.uk.)

About halfway along the bridge is the entrance to the **Tower Bridge Exhibition.** A visit takes you inside the bridge itself to see the original Victorian engine rooms and steam-driven machinery of the bascules. You can also walk across the high-level walkway and experience London and the river through its glass floor (if you have a head for heights!).

Tower Bridge

When the Pool of London was thriving in the first half of the 20th century, the bridge's bascules would have been raised about 5,000 times each year. At that time the waters in front of the Tower of London were jam-packed with sailing vessels – rowing boats, wherries, lighters and cargo ships – and it was said that you could actually cross from one side of the river to the other by leaping from boat to boat. Nowadays, Tower Bridge is the main crossing between the north and south bank of the river. Stroll across the bridge and you will be rewarded with stunning views of both the Square Mile and the Tower of London.

TOWER OF LONDON

The fortress was first constructed in the late 11th century, shortly after William of Normandy acceded to the throne, and at the time was the City's tallest, strongest and most fearsome building, built to intimidate both Londoners as well as invaders from the river. Its main keep, the White Tower, is over 30 m (98 ft) tall and has walls as thick as 5 m (16 ft) in places. Successive kings built further defences, towers and a moat, giving us the site we have today. Officially called Her Majesty's Royal Palace and Fortress, the Tower of London, it is nowadays designated a UNESCO World Heritage Site.

From the start, the Tower demonstrated the power and might of the king; it was not just a royal palace but housed the public records, Armoury, Treasury, Royal Mint, an observatory, prison, menagerie, the royal wardrobe and Crown Jewels. The latter are still kept in the fortress and are on daily view to the public in the Jewel House. They have been worn or used at coronation ceremonies since the

Tower of London

1660s and are totally priceless, containing some of the world's most magnificent diamonds, including the Cullinan I and II and the Koh-i-Noor. A visit to see them is sure to impress but queues are quite common, as this is one of the Tower's main attractions and draws crowds of visitors.

Many stories are told about prisoners kept in the Tower throughout its 900-year history, and of torture and royal executions. In fact, only ten executions were carried out within the castle walls on Tower Green and three of these were Tudor queens. For the most part, hangings and executions took place outside the Tower at Tower Hill. Prisoners would be taken to their trial by boat along the river and escorted by guards, leaving and returning to the Tower via Traitor's Gate. It must have been a terrible experience and even worse on the way back once sentence had been pronounced.

Nowadays, there are no human prisoners in the Tower but there is a resident community living on the site, consisting of the Resident Governor, a chaplain, a doctor and the Beefeaters (the Tower's Yeoman Warders). These ex-soldiers are easy to recognise throughout the grounds by their striking dark blue and red 'undress' (less formal) uniforms and are very much the ceremonial guardians of the Tower, keeping guard over the priceless Crown Jewels. In times gone by, they also guarded prisoners (mainly political) within the fortress. Every day they give tours of the Tower, delighting visitors with their breathtaking stories, and in the evening they participate in the Ceremony of the Keys – a ritual that has been taking place here for more than 700 years – when the Tower is locked up for the night. In addition, the Yeoman Warders will carry out state duties: at the annual Lord Mayor's Show, the coronation of a new monarch and at lying-in-state occasions. Much speculation exists about their name; it is generally believed that they were dubbed Beefeaters because, as members of the royal bodyguard, they were permitted to eat as much beef as they wanted from the sovereign's table. Another theory suggests that they were given the beef as part of their salary. Either way, the name stuck!

Until the mid-19th century, Beefeaters bought their position but since then they have to have served as senior non-commissioned officers in the armed forces for at least 22 years with an honourable record. Today, there are 37 Yeoman Warders at the Tower and only two of them are women. Detailed information about the Tower of London, the opening hours and entrance fees can be found on the Tower's website (www.hrp.org.uk).

Just a short walk along Lower Thames Street will bring you to:

CUSTOM HOUSE

There has actually been a Custom House on or near this site for 600 years and throughout its existence this building has been the scene of great activity. Since feudal times, kings would raise monies (to dispense justice, fund wars and run the country) by charging merchants for importing and exporting goods. Over the years, more and more duties were introduced, which resulted in the stretch of water immediately in front of Custom House being filled with ships of all shapes and sizes waiting to pay their dues.

The present elegant Georgian building dates from the early 19th century and was designed by David Laing and, later, by Sir Robert Smirke after part of it collapsed. It is the fifth building to have been constructed on the site and, although it is no longer used to collect taxes from boats arriving in the City, Her Majesty's Revenue and Customs continue to occupy offices within the premises.

The highlight of the building is its magnificent neoclassical room known as the Long Room. Its name was originally coined in 1671 by Sir Christopher Wren and it was subsequently applied to the public room of customs houses around the world, regardless of their shape or size!

At 58 m (190 ft) in length, Sir Robert Smirke's 1825 Long Room certainly lives up to its name. Throughout the 19th century, it was the place where all London customs business took place and was an enormously busy and lively space. Clerks lined the counter, processing goods' clearance for merchants, captains and brokers. All cargo ships entering the Thames were required to pay Customs duties before their merchandise could be unloaded or sold. Records show that there could be as many as 40 ships at any one time outside the Custom House. The cargo of every ship was weighed, measured and examined and Customs officers then assessed how much duty was to be paid. Only after payment was a release certificate issued that allowed the cargo to be sold. Forging certificates was punishable by death.

The Long Room was, in effect, the very first trading floor in London, for it was here that the captains would sell their cargo as soon as they had acquired their release certificate. Business was conducted in every language and local traders would have added to the hustle and bustle by coming up from the streets and selling their wares too.

Very close by the Custom House was a water gate on the Thames that became known as **Billingsgate**. With a deep, recessed harbour, this was an ideal place for goods to be loaded and the dock and roads nearby became the site of a general market from the 14th century. At that time a variety of produce was on sale, including foodstuffs, raw materials such as coal and iron, wine, salt and even pottery. It wasn't until the 16th century that it became almost exclusively a fish market.

An Act of Parliament was passed in 1699 making it 'a free and open market for all sorts of fish whatsoever'. The only exception to this was the sale of eels, which was restricted to Dutch fishermen whose boats were moored in the Thames. This was because they had helped feed the people of London during the Great Fire of 1666.

Although stalls and sheds surrounded the Billingsgate dock selling fish and seafood until the mid-19th century, in time it became obvious that a purpose-built market was required. In 1850, the first **Billingsgate Market** building was

Old Billingsgate Market

constructed on Lower Thames Street but was demolished in 1873 to make way for the present grand-arcaded market hall, designed by Sir Horace Jones and opened in 1876. Just over 100 years later, Billingsgate Market relocated to Docklands from its site in the Square Mile and the building then underwent a major refurbishment carried out by renowned architect Richard Rogers. Today, retitled **Old Billingsgate**, it has been reinvented as an entertainment venue, hosting many prestigious events ranging from international product launches to fashion shows. It has three key spaces – the Grand Hall, the Vault and the Gallery – and these are not only hired out for events but also for filming.

The exteriors (both river and road frontage) of the building are quite striking and it is certainly worth taking time to walk around the building's perimeter to examine its features, statues and architecture up close. Alternatively, Old Billingsgate and Custom House can be viewed from nearby London Bridge.

FIRE IN THE SQUARE MILE

BOUDICCA AND THE RAVAGING OF LONDON, AD60

On his death in AD59, Prasutagus, King of the Iceni tribe of Norfolk, left his kingdom to be shared equally by his family and the Emperor of Rome, in the expectation that the latter would protect and continue his dynasty. Emperor Nero, not satisfied with a mere half of the estate, took it all and then publicly humiliated Prasutagus's queen, Boudicca, by flogging her and raping her two daughters. She was so incensed by such treatment that she rose in revolt, along with a neighbouring tribe, the Trinovantes of Essex, first wreaking revenge on the city of Camulodunum (Colchester). She then moved on to Londinium, which she pillaged, looted and burned down, killing it is said, the majority of its citizens. The city had been left totally unprotected by the Roman governor, happy to leave people to their fate when he realised that he didn't have sufficient forces to withstand Boudicca's vengeful attack.

In recent years, archaeologists digging beneath London's streets have discovered a layer of reddish soil, along with burned buildings, clay and pottery shards – all evidence of Boudicca's scorching of the city. Some of these finds are today on view in the Roman gallery at the Museum of London (www.museumoflondon.org.uk).

Boudicca and the Iceni continued their rampage into St Albans and were then pursued to the Midlands by the Roman governor Paulinus and his soldiers. Totally defeated, Boudicca committed suicide and there are many myths as to how she took her life and where she was finally buried.

GREAT FIRE OF LONDON, 1666

The fire broke out in the early hours of 2 September 1666 in Thomas Farriner's bakers' shop in Pudding Lane, close to the wharves and warehouses lining the Thames. The mayor, Thomas Bludworth, was immediately informed about the fire and its dangers but, according to the famous diarist Samuel Pepys, he appeared unconcerned at the time and scathingly pronounced, 'Pish! A woman might piss it out.'

Initially, the fire caused little alarm, as fires were a common occurrence in a crowded city of narrow streets, where the main building materials were timber, wattle and daub. However, this one was fanned by unusually strong south-easterly winds that spread the fire north and west at an alarming pace. Unfortunately, the summer had been very dry and this made matters worse. Speedily, the fire spread through the riverside buildings that were full of combustible products such as oil, rope and timber, preventing access to the river (and the much needed water) to put out the flames.

The extent of the Great Fire of London within the City boundaries:
Roman and present

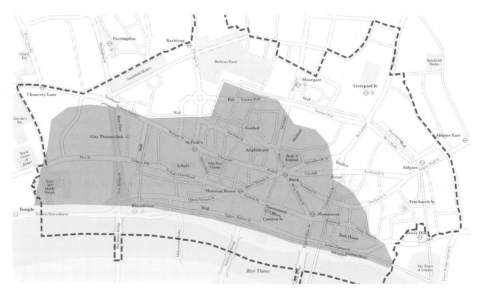

Pepys surveyed the fire from the tower of All Hallows by the Tower to see the progress of the blaze and then travelled to Westminster to inform the King about the extent of the fire in the city. On Pepys's suggestion, Charles II authorised the immediate demolition of buildings in the fire's path in the hope that this would slow down and eventually stop the inferno, but initial attempts did nothing to quell its growth.

Naturally, the city was in chaos as the medieval half-timbered buildings caught fire and people were forced out of their houses. Many Londoners abandoned their homes and fled to fields outside the City, such as Moorfields, where they took shelter. Some buried their possessions before leaving (Pepys wrote in his diary that he buried his wine and parmesan cheese in the garden); others crossed the river with as many of their belongings as they could carry. Unsurprisingly, people made money out of the situation – boatmen and coachmen pushed up their prices dramatically, making it impossible for many to use their services (although those who could afford the inflated fares managed to get away).

At the time, London had no organised fire service, so it was left to locals to douse the fire using buckets of water and water squirts; many attempts to stop the fire's path by introducing breaks between the houses were thwarted both on account of the fire being out of control and because of the strong winds. The fire raged for five days, during which time some 13,000 houses, 44 livery halls and 87 churches – including St Paul's Cathedral – were destroyed, and the Royal Exchange and Guildhall were very severely damaged. Ultimately, more than 100,000 people were made homeless and about 80 per cent of the city was devastated, necessitating massive reconstruction.

King Charles II and his brother James, the Duke of York (later James II), took control of the situation and managed ultimately to stay the course of the fire, which in time died out. London was in total ruin but work immediately began on reconstruction. Despite exciting plans proposed by Sir Christopher Wren to build a completely new city, one that would embrace wide boulevards, squares and new roads, the citizens wanted to return to what they had had before and so very quickly work began on rebuilding. New building regulations were introduced which decreed houses now had to be faced in brick instead of wood but, apart from this, the street layout and buildings were rebuilt much in the same fashion as before the Great Fire! It is possible to see sketches of Wren's plans in the Museum of London at Docklands. Certainly, the City proposed would have been utterly unlike what we have today, which is still based on the medieval street pattern with windy lanes, alleyways and narrow streets.

THE BLITZ, 1940–41

This was the name given to the concentrated bombing attacks that took place between September 1940 and May 1941 during World War II. During this eight-month period, enemy bombers dropped enormous amounts of explosives on London night after night, resulting in huge devastation and the deaths of around 15,000 people. The industrial areas around the docks and the East End were bombed repeatedly, buildings were set on fire and major transport hubs, landmarks (such as Buckingham Palace, St Paul's Cathedral and the City of London) suffered greatly too as they were easy to spot from the air. Many offices, warehouses and industrial premises went up in flames and more than 3.5 million homes were damaged. The area around St Paul's Cathedral was totally flattened, although miraculously the cathedral itself remained standing. Many of the 17th-century city churches suffered great devastation, losing their roofs, windows, pews, altars and much of their beautiful Wren interiors.

Londoners worked hard to put out the fires and clear the debris but the City had once again experienced horrific damage and hardship due to fire. In the postwar period, much reconstruction took place; churches were restored and rebuilt, new buildings were erected and ugly bombsites were converted into open-air spaces for people to enjoy. A good example of this is the church of St Dunstan-in-the-East that was transformed into a wonderful garden amidst the ruined church walls and tower.

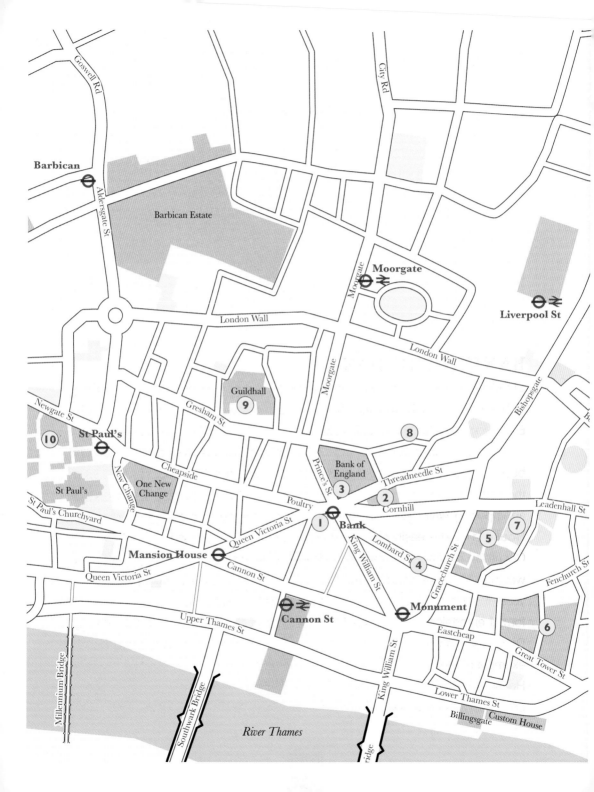

INSTITUTIONS, COMMERCE, BANKING AND FINANCE

*The walk starts outside exit 3 of **Bank underground station** (Central, DLR, Northern, Circle, District, Waterloo & City lines) in front of the Royal Exchange beside the Duke of Wellington statue.*

BANK JUNCTION

Standing on the terrace with your back to the portico entrance of the Royal Exchange, you might well feel that you are in the very heart of the Square Mile. Everywhere you turn is a major institution for which the City of London is known.

Six roads radiate from the junction ahead and this has always been a key and busy intersection throughout its history. The massive Bank of England sits to the north, to the right of the Royal Exchange and over to the left you will notice an imposing white stone building dominating the south side. This is **Mansion House [1]** and is easily recognisable by its blue railings, raised portico, imposing Corinthian columns and carved pediment. Extending over four floors, the house was built to be the official home of the Lord Mayor of London during the holder's year of office, with private apartments as well as sumptuous public rooms for formal entertainment. Designed by the Clerk of the Works to the City, George Dance the Elder (in the period 1739–52), this Grade I-listed building is a wonderful example of the architect's love of Palladian architecture and decoration. Mansion House is particularly renowned for the Egyptian Hall, with its many magnificent columns. Despite its name, the hall contains no Egyptian decoration and probably would be better named the Roman Hall, since it is based on Roman architect and writer Vitruvius' understanding of Roman buildings in Egypt.

Dance made provision for a number of state guestrooms on the first floor as well as a courtyard and designed a ballroom and hall balcony on the higher level. After his death, his son George Dance the Younger roofed over the courtyard to provide more space.

Beneath the building in the basement, Dance built a courtroom and 11 holding cells (including one called the 'birdcage' and used for women). It was down in the basement that the Lord Mayor, as Chief Magistrate of the City would preside over the court, trying cases and in the early 20th century that the women's rights campaigner and Suffragette leader, Emmeline Pankhurst, was incarcerated. The cells and courtroom are no longer in use and Mansion House today is where the Lord Mayor entertains visiting dignitaries, Heads of State, businessmen and senior politicians. The building is used for a vast range of official functions and it is here that the Chancellor of the Exchequer delivers his annual speech about the state of the British economy.

Guided tours take place every Tuesday afternoon and the building is usually open to the public during the London Open House weekend in September when visitors can marvel at Mansion House's particularly fine collection of 17th-century Dutch and Flemish paintings, including works of Jan Steen, Frans Hals, Aelbert Cuyp and Pieter de Hooch.

———————————————————————————————

Turn around to look at:

THE ROYAL EXCHANGE [2]

This is one of the City of London's most historically significant buildings, as it is on the steps of the Royal Exchange that the death of the monarch is announced and the accession of the new sovereign is proclaimed.

The present structure is the third to have been built on the site since its conception by Sir Thomas Gresham in 1566. It dates from the 1840s and has an imposing columned entrance inspired by the Pantheon in Rome. Above this portico within the triangular pediment, city merchants surround the central figure of Commerce – a testament to the enduring relationship between the building and the trade and commercial life of the Square Mile.

From Tudor times, the Royal Exchange has been a place where deals were negotiated and struck, and purchases made. Step inside now to see its luxury designer shops that line what was the original trading-floor space, or dine at its mezzanine-level Sauterelle restaurant or Grand Café in the colonnaded

The Royal Exchange

atrium. This is where City workers come to buy their watches, pens, jewellery, accessories, luxury cameras and clothing at Tiffany & Co., Hermès, Leica Camera Ltd, Smythson, Montblanc and Aspinal of London.

When the Royal Exchange was initially constructed 460 years ago, it had a trading floor and two higher floors that were leased out to individual shopkeepers. Up until this time trading had always taken place in the street, so this was a welcome change for the traders. In effect it was London's very first indoor trading and shopping mall.

The building has always had a great association with City institutions; initially the Stock Exchange operated from here, then Lloyd's of London (who remained for more than 150 years), and during the 1990s, LIFFE (London International Financial Futures Exchange) leased the building. Thanks to a major renovation in 2001, it looks like the Royal Exchange is set to remain a successful commercial establishment in the City for many years to come.

Now turn towards the left. Directly in front of you is:

THE BANK OF ENGLAND [3]

The Bank of England, was founded in the twilight years of the 17th century by the eminent Scotsman, City banker and trader Sir William Paterson (1658–1719). At the time, the country was at war with France and, through the Bank's establishment, much-needed funds and capital could be raised for the war effort. At first, the Bank leased premises from the Mercers' and the Grocers' Companies, but finally moved in 1734 into its own purpose-built home in Threadneedle Street. As the bank grew in size, larger premises were required and this led to Sir John Soane, the celebrated architect, becoming the Bank of England's official architect and surveyor. He began the Bank's extension and, for the next 45 years, work at the Bank remained his main concern. Apart from doubling the size of the building,

The Bank of England

he was also responsible for its very fine interior and for the introduction of a continuous windowless wall surrounding the Bank's premises to heighten security at the site.

Today, the building is still enclosed by Soane's wall, although most of the 'Old Bank' was demolished when Sir Herbert Baker (1862–1946) was given the task of designing a larger bank in the 1920s. Baker, who in the early 20th century had made his reputation creating great imperial buildings in South Africa and India, redesigned the building. He increased the Bank's height from three to seven storeys above ground and built three more in the basement making the Bank into the fort-like structure we see today.

The Bank of England is sometimes referred to as 'The Old Lady of Threadneedle Street', on account of a cartoon by James Gilray in 1797. It depicts Prime Minister William Pitt taking money from the coin-filled pockets of an old lady (representing the Bank), whose dress is made of £1 notes. She is seated on a locked chest full of money labelled Bank of England. Gilray's nickname for the Bank still remains and if you look above the main Threadneedle Street doorway you will see the aforementioned lady, still obvious in the pediment.

Nowadays, the Bank of England is not only the guardian of currency but is also the Government's banker and printer of banknotes. Since 1997, it has been responsible for setting interest rates and works independently of the Treasury. It holds the nation's gold and foreign exchange currency reserve and is said to be one of the largest reserves in the world, along with Fort Knox and the Federal Reserve Bank of New York.

At the time of printing, the Governor of the Bank of England is Canadian economist Mark Carney, who has been in the post since 2013. He is the first non-Briton to have held the post and also the most highly paid in the role! As the Bank's Governor and chair of the G20's Financial Stability Board, he is one of the country's most influential officials.

THE FINANCIAL CITY

Bank junction is aptly named, as the area is teeming with domestic and foreign-owned banks. In fact, the City of London has the greatest number of foreign banks (250) and the largest share in international bank lending throughout the globe, more than any other financial centre. It also boasts more head offices of banks than any other centre worldwide. Stroll around the area and you will immediately come across banks from Iran, Turkey, Saudi Arabia, China and Japan, as well as many European nations.

The City of London today is one of the world's top financial centres, alongside New York, Tokyo, Hong Kong and Singapore, and has the geographical advantage of being right in the middle of east and west time zones. With its enormous breadth of activities in the banking, insurance, foreign exchange, securities, derivatives and fund management industries, it has become the globe's foremost financial and related professional services centre. It is not only the European capital for private equity funds and hedge funds, but also trades almost twice as much foreign exchange as New York, its nearest rival, and is the world's main foreign exchange centre. It is now a leading base for Islamic finance and home to the world's first and only Sharia-compliant underwriting agency.

The eastern side of the Square Mile around Lime Street is where most of the insurance market is based. It is the world's leading market for internationally traded insurance and reinsurance and remains the only centre where all of the 20 greatest international insurance and reinsurance companies are active.

Turn round to face the traffic junction and cross over Cornhill on the left and take the first turning on the left into:

LOMBARD STREET [4]

On his arrival in 1066, William of Normandy (William I) brought with him a community of Jews who had helped make his homeland prosperous, acting as moneylenders and experienced in the ways of commerce. Many settled in the City in an area close by Lombard Street called Old Jewry. Although they continued their role as moneylenders to subsequent monarchs (who, like all leaders, were constantly in need of funds to pay for their buildings, wars and lavish entertainments), over the years the position of the Jews changed and many were reduced to poverty. As such, they were of little financial benefit to the king. In 1290, they were expelled from London by an Act of Parliament and their exodus made way for Italian Lombards to take over their moneylending role. The Lombards, who were licensed by the Pope to lend money, settled in the Square Mile in the mid-13th century after the Pope dispatched them to collect taxes owed to him.

Lombard Street was where they set up trade and they were easily identified by their 'bancas' (benches), where business was conducted. The street remained the leading centre for business dealings, negotiations, contracts and commerce up until the 1560s, when the Royal Exchange was built. The revolutionary construction

Signs in Lombard Street

of an interior trading floor meant that many merchants no longer wanted to trade out on the street and, as a result, the street lost much of its customer base.

Nonetheless, Lloyd's of London took up premises here from the late 1600s and stayed for the next 100 years. By the mid-19th century, Lombard Street had become famous as a street of banks. Barclays, Martins and Glyn, Mills & Co all had their head offices here. The Post Office headquarters were based here too. As you walk along the narrow medieval street today, look up to see the signs still hanging from its buildings. They are a wonderful reminder of its banking heritage.

Walk the length of Lombard Street and turn left into Gracechurch Street. Walk about 50 m (160 ft) and the entrance to Leadenhall Market is on the right-hand side of the street.

LEADENHALL MARKET [5]

Recent archaeological excavations have discovered that the present-day market is actually built over a former marketplace dating back nearly 2,000 years. For it was on this site that the Romans living in Londinium built their forum (marketplace) and basilica (city hall and law courts) in the 2nd century. At that time, it was the largest such site in the Roman Empire north of the Alps and spread over an area bigger than Trafalgar Square!

This is where business was carried out, deals were formed and merchants traded their wares. Much has been unearthed over the years, giving us an insight as to how the original Roman buildings were constructed and what they must have looked like. Mosaic pavements have been found as well as other artefacts from the Roman period, and are on display at the Museum of London.

Interestingly, the area was once again in use as a market in the 1300s; this time for poulterers and cheesemongers and continued selling these foods over the next century. When London was devastated by the Great Fire in 1666, the market buildings were badly damaged and had to be rebuilt. On reopening, it operated as a Beef Market, Herb Market and a Green Yard. During Victorian times, it became especially known for selling poultry, game, meat and fish. Today it is primarily a retail shopping and dining enclave.

Walk directly through the market and exit via Leadenhall Place into Lime Street. Turn right and then left into Cullum Street. Turn left into Fenchurch Street and right down Mincing Lane.

MINSTER COURT, MINCING LANE AND PLANTATION PLACE [6]

About 100 m (330 ft) on the left you will see the somewhat eccentric-looking pink marble edifice called Minster Court. Fans of Disney's 1996 movie *101 Dalmatians*

Minster Court

may well recognise the unusual neo-Gothic building as Cruella de Vil's fashion house, 'House of deVil'.

Minster Court is a complex of three buildings and home to the London Underwriting Centre (LUC) and other insurance companies. The LUC offers a meeting place for insurance company underwriters not part of Lloyd's syndicates to meet with other brokers in one location, sometimes hosting up to 4,000 broker visits in a day.

At the entrance to the main building, recognisable by its rather grand glass canopy, you will see three enormous bronze horses (the work of sculptor Althea Wynne) that have been nicknamed 'Dollar', 'Yen' and 'Sterling'. They are said to reflect the nature of the business carried out here and the prime financial trading centres of the world: New York, Tokyo and London.

Minster Court stands in a district once famed for its tea and spice trades. In the 1700s, it was also the heart of the British opium trade and was where 90 per cent of transactions took place. Just across the street was the site of Plantation House, the recognised centre of the tea trade in its day, now a substantial glass office block, Plantation Place. Because of its tea-trading activities, Mincing Lane ultimately became known as the 'Street of Tea'.

Today, Plantation Place's offices are used by a variety of insurance and consulting companies, including Accenture, Munich Re and QBE Insurance. A pedestrian route, Plantation Lane, has been built between its two buildings and is rather reminiscent of the ancient medieval alleys of the City. It is decorated on one side by Simon Patterson's wonderful piece of public art, *Time and Tide*, which brings London's rich and long history to life through text covering the ground.

Unusually, there is a public right of way through Plantation Place, providing a very useful short cut for office workers rushing about the City during their lunch break!

Plantation Lane

Walk up Plantation Lane, turn right at the church (St Margaret Pattens) and walk along Rood Lane. Cross over Fenchurch Street and then take the first right into Lime Street. Follow the windy road until you see the distinctive Lloyd's Building on your left.

LLOYD'S OF LONDON [7]

The Lloyd's Building is one of the City's most iconic – if not most controversial – buildings. Lloyd's of London moved to these premises in 1986, almost 300 years after it first set up business within Edward Lloyd's Coffee House in nearby Tower Street.

A global giant of the specialist insurance market, its name is recognised in every country of the world. For it is through Lloyd's that businesses and individual clients obtain insurance for risks, whatever their size or character, in return for the payment of a premium; the higher the risk, the costlier the premium set.

Lloyd's underwriters are renowned for their innovative skills and ability to solve difficult problems. Despite the company's early background in marine insurance, its breadth of risk coverage today is enormous, ranging from technological risks in the field of science, space and aviation through to risks involved in major

international sporting fixtures. In addition to its more conventional insurance, Lloyd's has been known to insure body parts – for example, a dancer's or sportsperson's legs (ballet dancer Rudolf Nureyev, Michael 'Riverdance' Flatley and football celebrity David Beckham), an opera singer's vocal chords, a food critic's tastebuds, a

Doorman at Lloyd's

musician's hands and an actress's breasts! When Richard Burton purchased a 69.42-carat diamond from Cartier for his wife, actress Liz Taylor, Lloyd's agreed to insure the jewel but with conditions attached. The ring in which the diamond was set could only be worn for 30 days a year and this had to be in the presence of security guards!

On a day-to-day basis, Lloyd's functions as a market, facilitating business in its Underwriting Room between underwriters (sellers) and brokers (buyers), who act on behalf of their clients (policyholders). Its origins date back to the mid-1600s at a time when Coffee Houses were all the rage. As in today's society, this was the place where businessmen and merchants would meet to discuss business and the affairs of the day. Edward Lloyd's Coffee House attracted in particular ship owners, ship captains, shipping merchants, and anyone with an interest in the marine industry and overseas trade would assemble here to hear the latest shipping news. So reliable was its information, Lloyd's ultimately became the recognised venue to obtain marine insurance.

By the end of the 18th century more spacious premises were needed, so Lloyd's moved into the Royal Exchange, where it stayed until the mid-1920s, and then bought its own premises in Leadenhall Street. It has continued to develop and grow, adapting and responding with great speed to changing circumstances, which is why it remains the world's leading specialist insurance market.

Cross over Leadenhall Street and turn left. Walk to the traffic lights and turn right into Bishopsgate. Turn left at its junction into Threadneedle Street. Where the road meets Old Broad Street, turn right into a passage between two office buildings (Threadneedle Walk). This leads to Throgmorton Street. About 50 m (160 ft) down on the right you will see a decorative doorway belonging to the Drapers' Company. A little further down you will come to some black iron gates (not open on weekends). Go through them into the passageway. The livery company building is on your right.

THE LIVERY COMPANIES AND THE CITY OF LONDON

From medieval times, 'Guilds' were a feature of the City of London and each guild controlled the provision of service and manufacture and selling of goods and food in the City. They prevented unlimited competition and helped to keep wages and working conditions steady in extremely unstable times. They protected their customers, employers and employees by monitoring inferior work that did not meet the standards set, was of bad quality or underweight! Fines and other penalties for selling bad food or shoddy goods could be severe – culminating in expulsion from the guild. This in effect meant that there would be a loss of livelihood, for it was impossible to work at a trade or sell goods in the City if you were not a member of a guild.

In order to become a member, you had to serve an apprenticeship that lasted seven years. The apprentice would be indentured to serve a master – a member of the guild – and during this time would often live in the master's household, learning the trade. At the end of the apprenticeship the apprentice could claim his freedom, which entitled him to serve under any master or to set up on his own.

The privilege of the 'freedom' was sought by all who wished to be successful in the City of London. With it the holder had advantages such as immunity from tolls at markets and fairs, freedom from being press-ganged into the Armed Forces and the right to vote at elections. This meant that the freeman had both trading rights and a voice in the government of the City. The entire municipal structure of London was built on the status of the freeman and even today freedom is a necessary qualification for the holding of a civic City office, such as Lord Mayor, Alderman, Sheriff or Common Councilman.

Over the years, the companies tended to acquire a permanent meeting place; initially, the mansions of rich citizens bequeathed to the companies; later, they were purpose-built halls and there are still many of these in existence today.

Although many have disappeared with the passage of time and various disasters, many have been rebuilt.

DRAPERS' COMPANY [8]

The Drapers' Company is one of more than 100 livery companies in the City, the first mentioned in records being the bakers and weavers in the 12th century. The Drapers received their initial Royal Charter in 1364 and the Charter of Incorporation about 75 years later. In the 16th century, the Lord Mayor established an Order of Preference for the companies and the Drapers were designated third in importance of the 12 Great Companies that dominated City affairs at the time.

Over the years, like many of the companies, they have accrued much wealth and property and their role has changed appreciably.

Nowadays, the Drapers' Company concentrates on charitable and educational activities, supporting all levels of education (primary, secondary and tertiary) in London and the United Kingdom. A good deal of its work focuses on enabling adolescents to study and gain qualifications in textiles to attain their full potential.

Drapers' Company

The Drapers made their money through the woollen cloth that was Britain's major trade in the Middle Ages. Their wealth is still most apparent inside their building, especially within their Hall, a truly sumptuous and quite magnificent chamber. One of the most opulent and richly decorated livery halls based in the Square Mile, the building was once the property of Thomas Cromwell, Earl of Essex, Chancellor to King Henry VIII and his right-hand man. After Cromwell's execution in 1540, his estate was taken over by the king and later sold on to the Drapers' Company for 1,800 marks (about £1,200). The house was destroyed in 1666, rebuilt and then underwent alterations during the Victorian era.

The interiors today are extremely lavish and explains why the Hall has been used as Buckingham Palace in films such as *Agent Cody Banks 2: Destination London* (2004). It also doubled as the Accession Council at St James's Palace in *The King's Speech* (2010), starring Colin Firth and Helena Bonham Carter, and appeared, using Russian interiors in *GoldenEye* (1995) and *The Saint* (1997). Not only a popular movie location the premises are regularly hired out for weddings, corporate hospitality, business dinners, meetings and banquets.

Return to Throgmorton Street, continue along Lothbury (with the Bank of England on your left) and walk directly along Gresham Street. Shortly on the right you will see an entrance into Guildhall Yard.

GUILDHALL AND GUILDHALL YARD [9]

For more than 800 years, the Guildhall has been the seat of government for the Corporation of the City of London. During that time, it has been the venue for coronation and jubilee lunches, the election of officials, political trials, mayoral installation ceremonies as well as the annual Lord Mayor's banquet.

It is remarkable that the 15th-century building's walls, crypt and porch have survived fairly unscathed into the 21st century, despite the ravages of major fire

Guildhall Yard

(1666) and aerial bombardment (1940). The building continues to function as the City's 'Town Hall' today.

Set back from Gresham Street within the surprisingly spacious Guildhall Yard, the building is well concealed and could easily be missed, yet once you stand in its grounds you are sure to be impressed by the quality of its medieval civic architecture. It is in fact, the only surviving secular stone building of its time in the Square Mile.

Completed during the reign of King Henry VI in 1428, the Guildhall was built by master mason John Croxton and today is a Grade I-listed building. The front porch was added towards the end of the 18th century and is used as the main ceremonial entrance. High above the entrance in front of the flagpole you can see the City of London coat-of-arms along with its motto: Domine dirige nos (Lord direct us).

The ancient building is flanked on both sides by 20th-century additions. To the east is the Guildhall Art Gallery, while the Court of Aldermen and Guildhall Library fill the western side of Guildhall Yard. Old and new are balanced all the more by St Lawrence Jewry church, which dates from the 17th century (although restored after World War II damage). The very beautiful church is now the official church of the City of London and used on many ceremonial occasions.

As you stand in Guildhall Yard, look out for a ring of black floor tiles. These represent the area of the Roman amphitheatre lying 6 m (20 ft) below ground that was found in the late 1980s. Access to the amphitheatre remains is via the Guildhall Art Gallery (see Chapter 11).

The Guildhall opens daily to the public between 10 a.m. and 4.30 p.m. (but is closed on Sundays from October to the end of April, and the Great Hall is closed throughout August). As it is sometimes used for state or civic functions, the building may shut at fairly short notice – so it is advisable to check online (www. cityoflondon.gov.uk) before you come. Entrance to the building is via the west door, near St Lawrence Jewry, and all visitors go through a security check before gaining access to the main Guildhall building.

THE GREAT HALL

The first thing that you notice is the sheer size of the hall. It is built like a cathedral and is one of the largest civic halls in existence in England today. It is here that many ceremonial events – including official dinners, receptions, banquets, Freedom of the City ceremonies, public addresses and the election of the Lord Mayor and Sheriffs – take place as well as regular meetings of the Corporation's elected assembly, the Court of Common Council.

Just inside the hall, at its west end, is the Minstrel's Gallery that contains enormous statues of the legendary giants Gog and Magog. These have a long association with the City and are supposedly mythical representations of a

Great Hall, Guildhall

pre-Christian struggle between Britons and Trojan invaders. The outcome of their conflict was the establishment of New Troy (now known as London). The giants, considered to be ancient guardians of the City, have been included in its parades since the early 1400s and still appear at the annual Lord Mayor's Show in November, although nowadays they are represented by wicker figures made by the Worshipful Company of Basketmakers.

Turn around to look at the full splendour of the hall. Around the walls there are decorative windows (restored after World War II) recording the names of all the Lord Mayors and their year of office. You will get an idea of the original Hall windows by looking at the 15th-century window on the south wall (by the Royal Fusilier memorial).

Up above, the stunning oak-panelled roof is the fifth to have been placed on the medieval walls. Beneath it you will notice a row of hanging banners. These

Gog

belong to each of the Great Livery Companies and are suspended over an attractive frieze that illustrates the arms of England, the City and the Twelve Great Livery Companies. The Great Hall would have been richly decorated when it was first built and it is still possible to see smidgens of gilding and paintwork on some of the stonework. Both the north and south walls are lined with monuments to national heroes and politicians, such as Admiral Horatio Nelson, the Duke of Wellington and Sir Winston Churchill – fitting in a Hall that has so often been the setting for the honouring of statesmen and world leaders.

In the 16th century, at a time of great political turmoil, it was in the Great Hall that two High Treason trials were held: one for Lady Jane Grey, the nine-day queen, and the other for Archbishop Cranmer. In both instances, the court pronounced the death sentence. Jane was to be beheaded and the Archbishop was to be hung, drawn and quartered. Nowadays, the Great Hall is the venue for the bestowing of the Honorary Freedom and for state celebrations, concerts, talks and meetings, and in September for the election of the new Lord Mayor. It is also where the Silent Ceremony takes place (see the panel below).

Beneath the Great Hall is the fabulous medieval undercroft, which is one of the City's hidden gems. As it is used for functions and events, it is not always available for viewing – but certainly worth a visit if it is open. The space is shared between

Guildhall Crypt

two crypts, both extremely atmospheric and quite ancient. In fact, the western crypt is said to predate the Great Hall above it. Having vanished for about three centuries, it only came to light again in the 1970s when major restoration work was being carried out.

Exit Guildhall Yard beside the entrance to St Lawrence Jewry church into Gresham Street and take the 4th turning on the left, Foster Lane, down to Cheapside. Here you should cross the main street towards St Paul's Cathedral. Walk along beside the churchyard railings, keeping the cathedral and gardens on your left. Pass by the Chapter House on your right and then turn right under the archway, Temple Bar Gate, into Paternoster Square.

THE LONDON STOCK EXCHANGE [10]

The London Stock Exchange moved to its new home at 10 Paternoster Square in 2004 and shares its location with banks, stockbrokers and private equity companies such as the Bank of America, Haitong Securities and Charterhouse Capital Partners. The European HQ of Merrill Lynch is close by in Newgate Street.

The Stock Exchange is undoubtedly one of the City's most important financial institutions. It evolved gradually out of the 17th- and 18th-century coffee houses, when those involved in the early trading of stocks met at Jonathan's and Garraway's in Exchange Alley as well as in the Royal Exchange. By the beginning of the 1800s, the Stock Exchange established itself on its own site near the Bank of England, where it remained for over 200 years. This building was demolished in the 1960s and replaced by a much larger tower block, reflecting how much the Stock Exchange had grown over time. However, the dramatic reforms of 1986 (sometimes referred to as the 'Big Bang') that brought about the deregulation of the financial markets also brought an end to traditional open outcry trading, when the shouts of 'buy, buy, buy' and 'sell, sell, sell' would be shouted across the trading room. With the introduction of automated screen-based trading, needs changed and within 20 years the institution had moved to its new purpose-built premises in Paternoster Square.

It is a wonderful location, in the shadow of St Paul's Cathedral and yet so close to shops, cafes and restaurants that line the piazza and surrounding streets. Paternoster Square is often the focus for outdoor events and it is not unusual to see a large screen placed here for the broadcast of key sports events, such as tennis matches at Wimbledon, football or other international sporting competitions.

This concludes the walk around the institutions of the Square Mile and where you can find both refreshments and toilet facilities.

The London Stock Exchange

The closest underground station is St Paul's (Central line), just a short walk away at the top of Cheapside.

THE CITY OF LONDON CORPORATION AND THE LORD MAYOR

THE CITY OF LONDON CORPORATION

The City of London Corporation is the body that administers and governs the Square Mile, a role it has undertaken for more than eight centuries. Predating the British Parliament as the first democratic metropolitan authority, the Corporation remains the custodian of the City's interests and is responsible for its economy, arts facilities, planning, transport and a host of other services in keeping with those covered by London's other local authorities. Even though it covers the smallest area, the City of London Corporation is by far the richest authority and plays a huge role in London, in the United Kingdom and overseas. Its responsibilities extend to managing a number of open spaces, including Hampstead Heath and Epping Forest, managing five of London's bridges, two central London markets, the Barbican Centre, the London Metropolitan Archives, the Old Bailey, the Museum of London, the Guildhall Library, Heathrow Animal Reception Centre and the City Information Centre.

Not only does the Corporation govern the City of London, it also promotes and markets the City's international finance and business services throughout the world. On a day-to-day basis, the Corporation is governed through the Court of Aldermen and the Court of Common Council and presided over by the Lord Mayor.

Of the two, the **Court of Common Council** is the main decision-making body and directs the work of the City Corporation. Its 100 members are elected for a four-year term by 25 City wards, with each ward electing two or more councilmen depending on the size of the electorate. In many respects, the Court of Common Council works in a similar way to the House of Commons, although it has one major and unique difference in that its members are all non-party political.

Aldermen and Beadles attending the Spital Sermon

The **Court of Aldermen** has its roots in the 12th century and was responsible for most of the City's administration until the 15th century. Nowadays, it has more of an advisory role, with Aldermen serving on the Court of Common Council committees and taking on the role of trustee or governor in hospitals, charities and educational establishments associated with the City of London. They also become involved in the regulation and approval of new livery companies and in granting Freedom of the City to applicants. There are 25 members of the Court of Aldermen, each representing one ward in the Square Mile. They are elected every six years on a rolling basis and, as the City has relatively few residents (approximately 8,000) compared to City workers (more than 400,000), voting is cast through two groups: residents and businesses.

THE SHERIFFS

This is the City of London's most ancient office and preceded that of the Lord Mayor. Up until 1189, it was Sheriffs (or Shire-Reeves) who were the King's Representatives responsible for collecting taxes, royal revenues and administering royal justice. Today, Sheriffs still have an exacting role assisting the Lord Mayor in carrying out the mayoral duties both at home and overseas and they officiate at sessions in the Central Criminal Court at the Old Bailey. In addition, they undertake a number of many other, tasks which include deputising for the Lord Mayor as and when required.

The Lord Mayor of the City of London and entourage attending the Spital Sermon

Two Sheriffs are elected each year on Midsummer's Day (24 June, or the closest weekday). One is generally elected through the Aldermen and is known as the Aldermanic Sheriff. He/she will then be in line for election as a future Lord Mayor. The other is normally elected through the Livery and known as the Non-Aldermanic Sheriff. Although not common, there are times when two Aldermanic Sheriffs are selected so that there are sufficient suitable candidates in the pool to become Lord Mayor. Since the 14th century, it has not been possible to become Lord Mayor without having first served as an Aldermanic Sheriff.

THE LORD MAYOR OF THE CITY OF LONDON

The City of London has been governed by its own Mayor for more than 800 years. The first to be appointed was Henry FitzAilwyn in 1189. The early Mayors sometimes held office for a long period of time (in the case of FitzAilwyn, for 24 years), but nowadays the Lord Mayor is elected for a one-year term and by custom only serves once in the role.

Nearly 700 have held the title, the great majority of them men, although there have been two women in the post since the 1980s. While carrying out the duties of Lord Mayor, the incumbent presides over the Court of Aldermen and Court of Common Council and also becomes the Chief Magistrate of the City of London, Admiral of the Port of London, Trustee of St Paul's Cathedral, Rector of City University of London, President of the City of London Reserve and Forces and Cadets Association and manages Her Majesty's Commission of Lieutenancy for the City of London. The right of Londoners to elect their own Mayor stems from a Charter granted by King John to the City in 1215. The very same year Magna Carta sanctioned the City to retain all its ancient liberties.

The Lord Mayor is elected each year on Michaelmas Day (29 September, or the closest weekday). He or she will already have served as a Sheriff of the City

The Lord Mayor's Show, 2017

of London, and be nominated by the Aldermen, then elected by the Livery. The Lord Mayor-elect does not take up office until the second Friday in November at the Silent Ceremony. This is when the ceremonial regalia (seal, purse, mace and sword) are passed to the new Lord Mayor and no words are uttered except for a declaration.

The next day is witness to a wonderful and colourful extravaganza, the **Lord Mayor's Show.** This involves the Lord Mayor parading through the streets in a magnificent gilded carriage from Guildhall to the Royal Courts of Justice to swear allegiance to the sovereign. The Show then continues in a carnival like

The Lord Mayor's Show, 2011

atmosphere, with many individual floats (the word 'float' derives from the time when the procession was held in barges on the Thames), and lasts the best part of the day with a splendid firework display across the river in the early evening. Each Lord Mayor introduces a special theme for the Show and aims to raise money for his or her selected charities.

This ancient and important role is entirely non-political and throughout the year of office, the Lord Mayor acts primarily as an ambassador for both the City of London as well as Britain. The Lord Mayor's costs during the term of office for travel, entertainment and hospitality (including hosting banquets and dinners for visiting heads of state and foreign dignitaries) are paid for through the City's Cash endowment fund that has built up over eight centuries.

The job is extremely demanding; promoting the City overseas and throughout the United Kingdom. The Lord Mayor spends about one-third of the year travelling overseas and is a major spokesperson for the business and financial sector. He or she heads delegations of senior businesspeople abroad to meet business and civic leaders in other countries – aiming to increase British trade and to highlight the services, expertise and markets of the Square Mile.

Throughout the term of office, the Lord Mayor works closely with his or her counterpart in the Royal Borough of Westminster and also with the **Mayor of London**. The role of the latter is markedly different to that of the Lord Mayors. He or she is an elected politician who works with the **London Assembly** and is accountable for the strategic government of Greater London during a four-year term of office. It is the duty of the Mayor of London to establish plans and policies and set a budget for the whole of the capital. At the time of printing, Sadiq Khan is the current Mayor of London having been elected in May 2016.

The Lord Mayor's Show, 2017

Gardens by St Paul's Cathedral

CHAPTER 3

CITY GARDENS AND OPEN SPACES

It is truly remarkable that such a compact urban area boasts so many delightful enclaves devoted to gardens and open spaces. There are around 200 such spaces in the Square Mile today and each of them has its own character. You will find traditional gardens, parks, a burial ground, ruined churches, former churchyards, piazzas as well as riverside, lakeside and highway plantings. You will also see roof gardens in abundance on the top of many buildings – and although these are generally not open to the public, they are encouraged by the planning

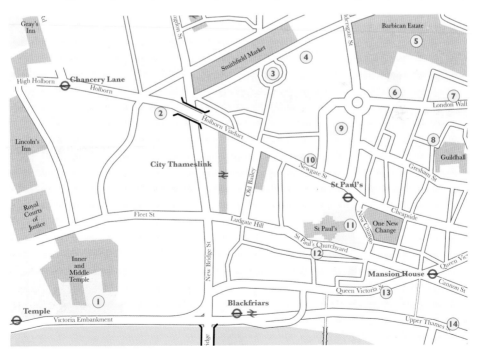

authorities to help improve the air and environment within the City. Wildlife such as insects and birds is now an enduring feature of many of the spaces and by careful planning and planting the gardens today offer improved wildlife habitats. Around the Barbican lakes you'll find mallards and moorhens, while peregrine falcons have been sighted on the City's tall buildings in recent times.

The Square Mile owes its abundance of green spaces largely to events in its past, namely the Great Fire of London in 1666 and the *Burial Act 1855* (this resulted in churchyards being closed down and their land becoming available for gardens). More recently, the devastating bombing of World War II created much derelict land.

Walk in the City any weekday lunchtime and you will see its workers taking advantage of these wonderful hidden corners. Often wedged in between towering blocks of offices, the green areas are surprisingly peaceful places, well equipped with wooden benches, flowers, shrubs and many long-established trees. In some you will find fountains or small ponds, monuments and sculptures or even parts of the Roman wall! Appealing to everyone, it is common to find tourists, families and even construction workers having a break in these green spaces. The walk outlined in this chapter introduces you to a variety of the spaces that exist in the Square Mile.

The walk begins at Temple underground station (Circle, District lines). On leaving the station, turn right towards the Victoria Embankment and then left into Victoria Embankment gardens. Exit at the far end, cross over Temple Place and turn left into a small passageway. Walk up a flight of stairs into Essex Street and at the junction with the Strand turn right. Walk along until you reach Prince Henry's Room (a Tudor-style, half-timbered building) and then turn right through the doorway. This leads down into the Temple area and the gardens stretch between the buildings of the Inns of Court and the River Thames.

TEMPLE GARDENS [I]

Located at the western boundary of the Square Mile, these little-known gardens are open to the public on weekdays between 12.30 p.m. and 3 p.m. Temple Gardens are situated in the very heart of legal London and shared between Middle Temple and Inner Temple, two of the four Inns of Court (*Chapter 7). The gardens have been here for centuries – possibly since the late 1100s, when the precinct was home to the Knights Templar – and they are a hidden oasis right in the centre of town.

Temple Gardens

Attractive manicured gardens surround the buildings and extend down towards the Victoria Embankment and River Thames. Middle Temple to the west is renowned not only for its lawns and flowers but also for Fountain Court, with its beautiful mulberry trees and tranquil central fountain. Inner Temple is particularly famous for its herbaceous borders, broad lawns, rose-beds, peony and woodland gardens. An orchard existed here in medieval times and, although it is now long since gone, the gardens still contain fruit trees: quince, mulberry and large-fruiting walnut. The Broadwalk is lined with lofty plane trees planted in the 1870s that provide wonderful shade on a hot, sunny day.

It is in these very gardens that William Shakespeare staged the meeting between John Beaufort and Richard Plantagenet, when a red rose and a white rose were plucked, leading to the War of the Roses of the mid-15th century. You may well recognise the gardens, as both they and the Inns have been used as the backdrop in a number of films (*Chapter 6).

_____

Exit the Temple via Middle Temple Lane into Fleet Street. Turn right and cross at the traffic lights. Then turn into Fetter Lane. Walk until you reach the junction at Holborn Circus. The garden at St Andrew Holborn is on your right.

ST ANDREW HOLBORN [2]

The garden here is a welcome space in a somewhat urban setting situated beside a busy road junction. It sits in front of St Andrew Holborn, which was rebuilt after the Great Fire and again after the Blitz of World War II. Recently relandscaped, the garden has an abundance of seating and is an ideal place to meet friends, take time out and watch the world go by. Beautifully laid out on two levels with a central lawn, the garden has the most attractive willow tree and a good array of shrubs and flowers. It is a very popular venue and close to the diamond district of Hatton Garden.

Walk up the steps to Holborn Viaduct. Cross the road and turn right. Shortly there is a stairwell on the left. Walk down to Farrington Street, turn immediately left and then right into West Smithfield. Walk along the street with Smithfield Market on your left. The garden is in an island on the right hand side.

SMITHFIELD ROTUNDA [3]

This circular garden is unusual for the City in that it contains children's rustic play equipment. It is on the site of what has been an open space within the Square Mile since the 12th century and remarkably remains so still. Dominated in the centre by a bronze statue of Peace surrounded by water fountains, the garden is full of mature trees (including fig) and provides good shrub cover for nesting birds.

Considering the bloody history of the area (*Chapter 6), it seems ironic that the Rotunda is such a calm sanctuary today. It is very popular with local residents, office workers, tourists and those visiting St Bartholomew's Hospital, which is close by.

Exit the Smithfield Rotunda, turn right and then cross West Smithfield. Just after the turning to Cloth Fair, you will see a small half-timbered entranceway on your left. Go through the gateway and then turn left up a short flight of steps into the churchyard of:

ST BARTHOLOMEW THE GREAT [4]

Here we have another unexpected treasure tucked away from the noise and bustle of Smithfield Market and adjacent to St Bartholomew's Hospital. Take a seat in the raised garden (a former graveyard) and feast your eyes on the striking church building with its flint and stone facade. The garden is enclosed by buildings

St Bartholomew the Great's garden

on three sides and is atmospheric, with several headstones propped up around the walls.

The church was originally built as part of a priory in 1123 by Rahere, a courtier of King Henry I. Having survived a terrible illness while on pilgrimage to the Holy Land, Rahere vowed to set up a priory and hospital on his return home to mark his recovery. He founded both in the 12th century and although the priory thrived, it was closed down during the Dissolution of the Monasteries in the 1530s. It reverted to use as a parish church during the reign of Queen Elizabeth I (in the mid-16th century) and it is now regarded as London's oldest parish church with a long and fascinating history.

Retrace your steps through the gateway and turn right towards the market buildings. Turn right into Long Lane and walk to the end of the street. Barbican underground station will be on your left and you will see the Barbican Estate directly in front of you. You need to walk through the tunnel ahead to reach the main entrance to the Barbican Centre.

BARBICAN CENTRE: LAKES, CONSERVATORY, GARDENS [5]

The Centre, built as part of the Barbican Estate in the 1960s and 1970s, is renowned for its beautiful water features, lake, fountains and gardens, which are extremely well tended by the Corporation of London's gardeners. The Centre's

Barbican lake and plaza

main foyer leads out onto the lake terrace. Here you can sit and watch wildlife, birds and ducks on the water or perhaps eat lunch on a warm day. Nearby, interspersed amid the grass and flower borders, you can see parts of the 2nd-century Roman wall from where the name Barbican was derived.

Barbican Conservatory

On Level 3 of the main Arts Centre is the **Barbican Conservatory,** which is London's second-largest conservatory and an absolute delight. It was built to disguise the fly tower of the Centre's theatre and its walls are covered with plants from all over the world. It is a truly tropical garden, with over 2,000 species of plants and trees as well as exotic fish. Open on Sunday and Bank Holiday afternoons between 12 p.m. and 5 p.m., it is certainly worth a visit and you can even book a table for afternoon tea within the garden (there are three sittings between 12 p.m. and 4.30 p.m.). If you want to find out more about the plants and history of the garden, book a place on the free tour of the Conservatory given by resident gardeners at 11 a.m. when the Conservatory is open.

The Barbican is full of green spaces; to the south, by London Wall, you find the **Barbers' Physic Garden** [**6**], which was built on the site of the 13th of 21 bastions constructed in AD122 by Emperor Hadrian. There has actually been a garden on this site for more than 460 years! The present garden dates from 1987 and is full of plants that have been used in medicine and surgery as well as for domestic purposes over the centuries. Nearby, a new destination, **London Wall Place** [**7**], has been developed which incorporates remains of the Roman city wall and a medieval church and has been landscaped with gardens, water features as well as a high walkway. Roof gardens have been established too that give great views of the area below as well as over the city.

_____

Due to the construction of Crossrail, the area surrounding the Barbican Estate may be difficult to navigate. Exit the Barbican at its main entrance on Silk Street and turn right. Turn right again at the junction with Moor Lane. At the next junction (Fore Street) turn right and follow the road as it bears left into Wood Street. Cross over the main road, London Wall, and continue along Wood Street. Pass by the City Police station on your left and then take the next turn left into Love Lane. Walk for 20 m (65 ft) and you will reach:

ST MARY ALDERMANBURY [8]

This garden is dominated by a plinth with a bust of William Shakespeare and commemorates two of his fellow actors, Henry Condell and John Heminge, who are buried in the churchyard. It is due to their endeavours as coeditors of Shakespeare's plays that Shakespeare's First Folio was printed. The men are famed for having divided Shakespeare's plays into histories, tragedies and comedies and it is said that their work in printing the First Folio meant that the plays which had not been previously printed (such as *Macbeth*, *Twelfth Night* and *The Tempest*) were ultimately saved after his death.

Bust of Shakespeare

Another feature of the garden is the remains of the church of St Mary Aldermanbury, now filled with a lawn and flowerbeds. A City church that was rebuilt by Sir Christopher Wren after the Great Fire in 1666, it was badly hit in the Blitz of 1940 and the ruined area was later laid out as a public garden.

Retrace your steps along Love Lane. Cross Wood Street and walk straight ahead under the office building. Walk up a short flight of steps and bear left. At Noble Street, turn left and then turn right into Gresham Street. At the next junction, turn right and cross the street at the traffic lights beside St Botolph's church. Enter the park to the left of the church.

POSTMAN'S PARK [9]

In the late 19th century, the southern boundary of the gardens was home to the headquarters of the General Post Office. At that time, many postmen would come to the park in their work breaks and this led to the nickname 'Postman's Park'. The park had opened in 1880 on the site of the former churchyard of St Botolph's, Aldersgate, and was enlarged in the next decade when it took over the disused burial grounds of two local parishes. Today, it is a stunning green haven between King Edward Street and Aldersgate Street. If you look carefully, you still see evidence of its past around the park walls and railings with remnants of some very old gravestones.

Apart from its name and delightful setting, this small park is quite unlike any other in the Square Mile on account of its very moving memorial cloister – a 15 m (50 ft) gallery with a tiled roof. The cloister owes its existence to the eminent Victorian artist G.F. Watts, who built it to commemorate the Diamond Jubilee of

National Memorial to Heroic Self Sacrifice

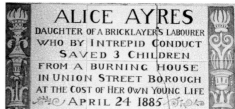

Plaque to Sarah Smith   **Plaque to Alice Ayres**

Queen Victoria in 1897. Officially entitled the 'National Memorial to Heroic Self Sacrifice,' the cloister contains a number of decorative ceramic and glazed tiles on its back wall recording the stories of ordinary men and women who lost their lives carrying out acts of heroism. There are moving tales of rescues made on the River Thames, from house and work fires, on broken ice, in quicksand and from runaway horses. Death due to fire and drowning are sadly the main themes and it is not unusual for the plaques to contain motifs representing the manner in which life was lost.

In all there are 54 plaques, each one describing fearless and courageous deeds, and they are very poignant to read. The one marking the earliest event describes Sarah Smith, a pantomime artiste, who lost her life in 1863 while attempting to douse flames that had covered her companion.

Another tells the 1885 story of Alice Ayres: 'Daughter of a bricklayer's labourer who by intrepid conduct saved 3 children from a burning house in Union Street Borough at the cost of her own young life'. The most recent plaque was added in 2009 and is dedicated to Leigh Pitt, a print worker who lost his life in 2007 after saving a drowning child from the canal.

Leave the park through the western gate on King Edward Street and turn left. Cross the road at the junction with Newgate Street and walk into the ruined church garden.

CHRISTCHURCH GREYFRIARS CHURCH GARDEN [10]

Here we have yet another unusual garden, enclosed by the former church walls and tower. When the interior of the church was devastated by enemy bombing in December 1940, leaving only the tower standing, the decision was made not to rebuild the church. Subsequently, the Corporation of London converted it into a garden so that it could be of benefit to Londoners, local office workers and visitors to the City.

The transformation has been cleverly executed so that the nave has become a rose garden; paths have replaced the former church aisles. There are wooden towers where the church pillars once stood, while box hedging represents the

Christchurch Greyfriars Church Garden

church pews. Despite being located alongside a busy and noisy road, the garden itself is most peaceful and boasts a wonderful display of seasonal flowers during the spring and summer months.

Now, cross over Newgate Street and head left. Pass the entrance to St Paul's underground station and walk into St Paul's Cathedral gardens.

ST PAUL'S CATHEDRAL, FESTIVAL AND JUBILEE GARDENS [11]

This is the ideal spot to relax after sightseeing in the cathedral or visiting the Tate Modern art gallery on the south bank of the Thames. There are several areas of gardens: the main lawn is on the south-east side of the cathedral, the Festival

St Thomas Becket

Gardens are just outside the cathedral precincts and beside them are the Queen's Diamond Jubilee Gardens (all on the south side).

You will find benches in each of the gardens along with sculptures, flowers and shrubs. The main cathedral gardens are best for shade, as they have large trees (a London plane, two ginkgos, a giant fir and even a katsura). Here you will also find a rose garden and an interesting modern sculpture of St Thomas Becket by Edward Bainbridge Copnall. Becket appears to be in pain while fending off an attack, possibly the blows of the four knights responsible for his death.

Leaving the main cathedral gardens via the iron gate, you see the **Festival Gardens** to your left just by the junction of New Change and Cannon Street and the **Queen's Diamond Jubilee Gardens** to your right. The Festival Gardens were built on derelict bomb-damaged land after World War II, and have won many awards for their flowers and plants. Laid out around a sunken lawn with a wall

Festival Gardens

fountain (the gift of the Worshipful Company of Gardeners), the area was once the site of the Cordwainers' Hall.

The Queen's Diamond Jubilee Gardens were opened in 2012 and have greatly enhanced the space around St Paul's Cathedral. The beautifully manicured lawns, low hedges, herbaceous planting and public art have become a real focal point of the area. Sculptures here include a memorial to the poet John Donne, who was Dean of St Paul's Cathedral in the early 17th century, as well as a stainless steel spherical work of art, *Amicale*, by Paul Mount (1922–2009).

Just across the street you will see a striking modern glass-fronted building that houses the **City Information Centre [12].** Designed by Make Architects, the building is triangular in shape and almost looks as though it has outstretched arms to welcome visitors. Since its arrival here in 2007, it has become a real landmark in the area and has won a number of architectural awards.

The highly trained assistants are multilingual and give help, advice and information about all areas of London. Staff can also organise hotel reservations,

City of London Information Centre

sightseeing tours, theatre tickets and foreign exchange. The centre stocks free brochures as well as maps, guidebooks and Oyster cards. Outside is the small landscaped garden of Carter Lane, an ideal spot to sit and take in the magnificence of the cathedral and its precincts.

Turn right into Peter's Hill, with the Millennium Bridge in front of you. When you reach Queen Victoria Street, turn left. About 100 m (330 ft) along you will see Cleary Garden on your right.

CLEARY GARDEN [13]

The garden commemorates Fred Cleary, who was responsible for the creation of many new gardens in the Square Mile during the 1970s. It is built on three levels, each with its own character. This is an ideal place to take time out and is especially beautiful in spring, when the Japanese peonies are in bloom. There are many shaded benches, wooden arbours as well as a lawn. A tiny vineyard on the terrace marks the area's former existence as a centre of the wine trade in the Middle Ages. During recent excavations, Roman baths have been discovered at the southern end of the garden.

Exit the garden and turn right onto Queen Victoria Street. Turn right beside Mansion House underground station into Cannon Street. Take the 2nd turning on the right, College Hill. Walk to the road junction with College Street and cross the road into:

WHITTINGTON GARDEN [14]

Just a stone's throw away from the church of St Michael Paternoster Royal, this garden is named after famous four-time Mayor of London Dick Whittington

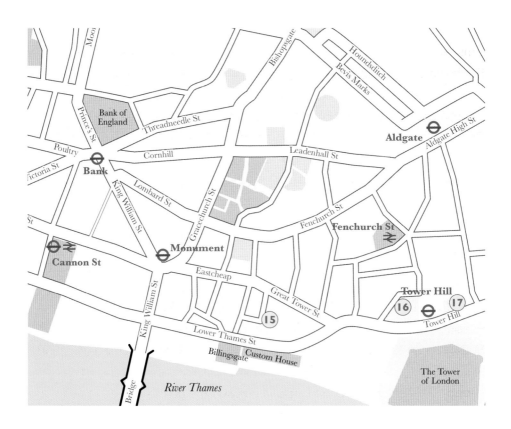

(c.1354–1423). Many stories are told about him, some more myth than real, but he was known to be a great philanthropist and financed many public projects. Examples of his generosity include paying for the rebuilding of the Guildhall and his parish church (St Michael Paternoster Royal), for improvements to be made to drainage systems across London and for the implementation of public sanitation. He is also remembered for helping to improve the plight of apprentices and unmarried mothers.

On his death, £7,000 was left to charity in his will (about £3 million in present-day money), which helped to build the first library at the Guildhall, paid for almshouses, contributed to the rebuilding of Newgate Prison and the repair of St Bartholomew's Hospital.

The garden is a quiet and formal space with benches, a fountain and a pair of unusual sculptures: two herdsmen on horseback, seated on granite stands. Designed by Italian sculptor Duilio Cambellotti (1876–1960), they were a gift to the City from the Italian president on his state visit in 2005.

The quickest way to reach the next stop is to walk east along Upper Thames Street. Continue after London Bridge into Lower Thames Street and turn left up St Dunstan's Hill. The garden is right in front of you.

ST DUNSTAN-IN-THE-EAST [15]

Possibly the most scenic and atmospheric of all the City of London gardens, St Dunstan-in-the-East was established in the late 1960s in the ruins of a church that had been devastated during World War II. Only the walls and Christopher Wren's 17th-century tower and steeple survived the bombing of 1941 and these

still act as a dramatic backdrop to the delightful garden. Very popular all year long, St Dunstan-in-the-East is built on two levels and renowned for its beauty and serenity. There are creepers and ornamental vines, wonderful mature trees, exotic plants and a Japanese snowball beside the fountain that has magnificent blossoms during spring.

St Dunstan-in-the-East

Turn left out of the gardens into St Dunstan's Hill. At the junction turn right onto Great Tower Street. Walk along, passing by the church of All Hallows by the Tower on your right, and then turn left into:

TRINITY SQUARE GARDENS AND WAR MEMORIAL [16]

Although this area is not actually within the confines of the Square Mile, it is such an important part of London's history that it really cannot be omitted. The extremely manicured and well-tended gardens are sited on Tower Hill, opposite the Tower of London, and for many years this was a place of public execution. From the 14th to the 18th century, the Tower Hill scaffold was a common sight and many well-known figures – such as Sir Thomas More, Bishop John Fisher, George Boleyn (Ann Boleyn's brother), Thomas Cromwell and two Archbishops of Canterbury – lost their heads here.

On execution day, the area was mobbed with crowds of people and temporary seating had to be erected to allow citizens to view the gruesome proceedings. Often constructed in a hurry, this seating was known to have collapsed on several occasions causing even more loss of life!

Today, a small memorial to those who were executed here is sited in the west of the gardens and nearby there is a touching memorial cloister to the Merchant Seamen who lost their lives during the two World Wars of the 20th century. It is

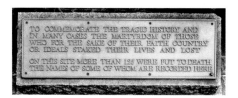 

Plaques at the ancient execution site on Tower Hill

a very special place that is both full of history and stocked with fine trees, lawns, plants and flowers.

Exit Trinity Square Gardens via the east gate, walk past Tower Hill underground station and follow the path until you arrive at:

TOWER HILL GARDEN [17]

Situated directly opposite the Tower of London, this garden encompasses part of the 2nd-century Roman wall and boasts an exceptional view of the Tower. It is well landscaped and ideal for children and families, as it has excellent children's play equipment.

With lawns, trees and seating, it is a great place to chill out and relax at the end of your City Gardens tour.

Tower Hill underground station (Circle, District lines) and Tower Gateway (Docklands Light Railway [DLR]) are both nearby.

Tower Green gardens

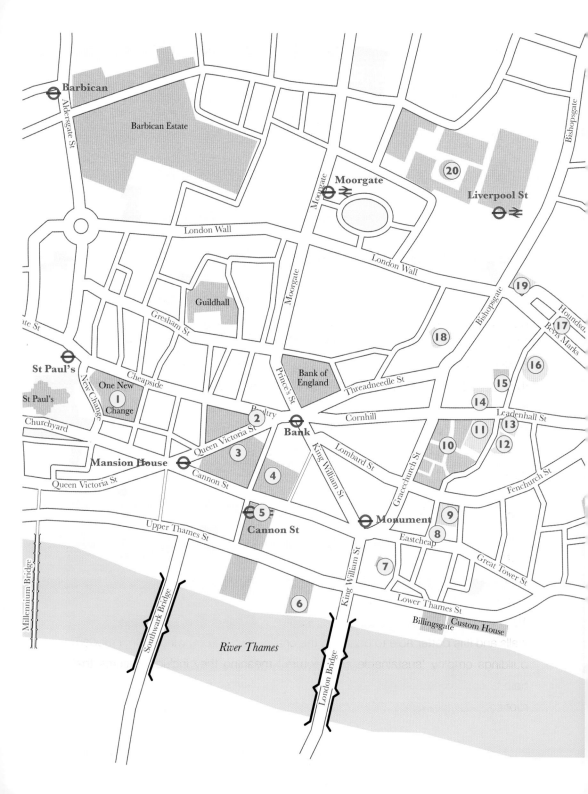

CHAPTER 4

DESIGN AND ARCHITECTURE
IN THE CITY OF LONDON

Since Roman times, the architecture of the Square Mile has always reflected its trades and day-to-day commercial life. Throughout its history, the City of London has suffered rampage, fire and great destruction yet it has always managed to bounce back, rebuild its fabric and move forwards. When nearly a third of the City was devastated during World War II, it left an array of empty spaces where businesses and houses had once stood. Postwar reconstruction saw many of these rebuilt, generally replacing former offices or housing stock, but it was also an opportunity to introduce new ideas and designs. It is a trend that has continued to this day, making a visit to the City of London an architectural delight.

Walk along the City's streets and you will come across all manner of styles and age of buildings. See remnants of the ancient Roman wall, medieval churches, livery halls, Georgian terraced houses, alleyways concealing 17th-century pubs and taverns, Victorian office and commercial buildings plus the ever-growing cluster of high-tech and soaring office blocks in the City's EC2 and EC3 financial districts. Since the creation of the 'framed tube structure' in the late 20th century, we have seen more and more super-tall office buildings erected, far exceeding the height of the City's very first (and controversial) skyscraper, Tower 42, built in the 1970s. Now, new technology allows for greater window space and fewer interior walls and it is better able to deal with the challenge of strong winds. Most modern buildings employ 'sustainable architecture,' meaning they include features that help to conserve heat and energy; many integrate environmentally friendly 'green' roof areas and walls into their structures.

One of the features that makes the City so unique is its rich mix of architecture encompassing so many different styles. Not only do Christopher Wren's 17th-century buildings still dominate the Square Mile (seen in his wonderful legacy of St Paul's Cathedral and many City churches) but there are good examples too of the work of many 18th-, 19th and 20th-century architects, such as Sir John Soane, George Dance the Elder, William Tite, Sir Herbert Baker and Sir Horace Jones. As their buildings (such as the Royal Exchange, the Bank of England and Mansion House) are covered elsewhere in the book (*Chapter 2), they have not been included in this chapter, which is largely devoted to contemporary architecture within the Square Mile.

The closing years of the 20th century witnessed the arrival of an exciting new group of architects who have undoubtedly made their mark here. The influence of Richard Rogers and Norman Foster in particular should not be ignored. Both have been prolific and made a major contribution to City design. Rogers' buildings are highly recognisable thanks to his use of primary colours and the positioning of lifts and pipes on the exterior surfaces (for example, The Lloyd's Building, 88 Wood Street and The Leadenhall Building), while Foster is celebrated for his curvy designs, notably for 30 St Mary Axe (aka The Gherkin), Willis Building and The Walbrook. The work of other celebrated British designers – such as Terry Farrell, Nicholas Grimshaw and Michael Hopkins – is also highly evident in the City's streets and each has his own distinct style.

Due to the stature of the City internationally, it is not surprising that esteemed architects from all over the world have contributed to its current fabric and skyline. Just walk the streets to see the amazing architecture of Rafael Viñoly, Jean Nouvel and Rem Koolhaas in striking buildings around the Square Mile today.

The following architectural walk is a mere snapshot of what is on offer around the City's streets, as there is not enough room in this book for individual accounts of all the City's buildings. However, as mentioned earlier, details of a number of the properties can be found elsewhere within **Explore London's Square Mile** (for example, the City Information Centre highlighted in Chapter 3).

The Design and Architecture walk begins outside St Paul's underground station. Cross in front of St Paul's churchyard to the right-hand side of Cheapside. The shopping centre called One New Change is on the right, with an entrance about 30 m (100 ft) along Cheapside.

ONE NEW CHANGE [1]

This 2010 development has revitalised Cheapside, returning the street to its original medieval roots as a main shopping district. Jam-packed with shops, restaurants and cafes, it is a most welcome addition to the Square Mile. It is open seven days a week, making the City accessible both during the week and on weekends. The designer, Jean Nouvel, has cleverly demonstrated the connection of the building

One New Change

with its environs by positioning the mall's glass elevators in such a way that you witness the most wonderful view of the dome of St Paul's Cathedral as you ascend to the roof terrace. Here, you will find **Madison**, a popular venue for cocktails and fine dining but also an unexpected roof space giving superb panoramic views over the Thames, St Paul's Cathedral and the City. In summer, the terrace is set up for free screenings of the annual Wimbledon tennis tournament and hosts other events such as outdoor yoga classes.

Due to its multicoloured glass exterior with both clear and opaque panels (there are more than 6,300 in different shapes and sizes), the building's appearance seems to change throughout the day, which makes it all the more interesting. One New Change is quite unique within the Square Mile; it has brought vibrancy to the area around St Paul's Cathedral and provides a shopping experience that has not existed here for many years.

Exit the shopping centre on to Cheapside and turn right. Walk for about 200 m (650 ft) until Cheapside becomes Poultry. Towards the end of the road on the right is:

NO. 1 POULTRY [2]

One of the 20th century's most controversial buildings, this monumental pink and yellow edifice remains to this day a matter of debate. The development itself took 40 years to materialise and only then after public inquiries and a court case had given it the go-ahead. Designed in the postmodernist style by celebrated architect Sir James Stirling (1926–1992), who died five years before the building was completed in 1997, No. 1 Poultry is sometimes likened to a ship, with the building's stripes appearing to represent the decks on board. HRH Prince Charles has also described it as looking like a 1930s radio!

No. 1 Poultry

The building opens on two sides, connecting with both Queen Victoria Street and Poultry, has a hollow central atrium with offices above plus public space and shops at street and basement levels. The bar and restaurant on the roof are popular with the City workforce. (*Chapter 8).

In 2016, No. 1 Poultry was given a Grade II* listed status making it the most modern listed building in the entire United Kingdom. This confirms its importance as a major work of late 20th-century architecture by one of the country's most eminent postwar architects.

Cut through the ground floor atrium and exit to Queen Victoria Street. Bloomberg Place is immediately in front of you.

BLOOMBERG PLACE [3]

Designed by Foster + Partners and opened in 2017, this is the new headquarters of the financial and media empire run by Michael Bloomberg (ex-Mayor of New York). The height of the two interconnected buildings has been restricted to ensure that the buildings do not obstruct the view of St Paul's Cathedral (in line with the London View Management Framework guidelines), thus preventing the cathedral from losing its prominence on the London skyline and ensuring its protected view status.

Bloomberg Place covers an area that was once a major part of Roman London (*Chapters 1 and 11), and great care has been taken in the buildings' design to ensure that they respect their historic position within the Square Mile. Much attention has also been given to the materials used on the exterior to fit in with the medieval nature of the City.

Cross Queen Victoria Street, turn left and walk towards Bank junction. Turn into Walbrook, the first turning on the right, and walk to its junction with Cannon Street. The Walbrook building is on your left.

THE WALBROOK [4]

Taking its name from the now subterranean River Walbrook, this 2010 building is another of Foster + Partners' designs. Cross Cannon Street to see the full extent of the building and you can appreciate both its position on its site as well as its wonderful curves and exterior casing. Inside, there is a lofty glass-ceiling atrium through which light reaches the office space and trading floors. Shops and cafes face onto Cannon Street and Walbrook on the ground level, while the building skilfully curves around a church garden at the rear.

The Walbrook

Now look to your right:

CANNON PLACE [5]

Completed in 2011, Cannon Place is built not only above Cannon Street railway station but also upon what could be the remains of a Roman Governor's (or high-ranking official's) home and designated a Scheduled Ancient Monument. When the site was excavated in the 1990s, the Museum of London Archaeology (MOLA) discovered the remains of an elaborate building from the late 1st century/early 2nd century ad consisting of large reception rooms, some mosaic floors, a garden and pools. The purpose of the site is not entirely clear but there is speculation that it might have been used for administration or perhaps have included a Governor's or an official's house.

   The architects, Foggo Associates, took great care in their design for Cannon Place. They used a steel megastructure of long beams and girders to lessen

Cannon Place

the impact on the Roman artefacts below. Like much of the architecture in the area, the building is distinguished by its glass exterior; it also has a 'green' roof to minimise rainwater run-off and to provide a habitat for birdlife.

Turn down Dowgate Hill beside the station. At its junction with Upper Thames Street, turn left. Cross the road and turn right down Allhallows Lane. On reaching the riverfront, turn left. Riverbank House is just a few minutes' walk away.

RIVERBANK HOUSE [6]

Situated right beside the River Thames, David Walker Associates' 2010 building illustrates how the use of vivid colour (yellow) and the introduction of steel and glass balconies can make a building very striking. The extensive balconies ensure that the building manages to stand out from its surroundings and it is unlike most other City office buildings. Walk along the riverside path at night and see the glow from the building against the evening sky.

Riverbank House

Continue along the river path and turn left up Swan Lane. On reaching Upper Thames Street, turn right. Cross over the road at the traffic lights and walk up Fish Street Hill on the left. Shortly on your right you will see The Monument.

THE MONUMENT [7]

The Monument was erected as a memorial to the Great Fire of London of 1666 and was designed by Sir Christopher Wren and Dr Robert Hooke. An imposing Doric column made of Portland stone, it took six years to complete (1671–7) and remains the tallest freestanding column in the world to this day. Its height of 61 m (202 ft) represents the distance between the column and the baker's shop in Pudding Lane where the fire broke out on 2 September 1666. (*Fire in the Square Mile panel, Chapter 1).

The imposing column still acts as a reminder of the impact of fire on the Square Mile and of the new city that emerged from the ashes. Its gilded flaming urn is

The Monument

easily visible from the river and from many points within the City's streets. It is open to the public daily and you can climb the 311 steps of the spiral staircase to the summit, from where you get superb views of London (and will be given a certificate commemorating your visit).

If, however, you don't have a head for heights, take time to look at the panels on the pedestal at the base of the column that describe the event (in Latin, but with an English translation). They illustrate in wonderful bas-relief (the work of Caius Gabriel Cibber) the king, Charles II, consoling the ruined City (symbolised by the female figure).

When the column was erected, Wren built an underground laboratory down in the basement. His intention had been to perform scientific experiments here and to use The Monument itself as a giant vertical zenith telescope to measure the movement of the stars and Earth. However, the laboratory was ultimately

The Monument

abandoned in favour of a newly constructed observatory at Greenwich, as vibrations from the constant stream of traffic surrounding The Monument interfered with the success of Wren's and Hooke's work.

Although the room has not been open to the public for many years, there are plans now to build a visitor centre at the bottom of The Monument that would allow visitors to view the 17th-century laboratory. The City of London Corporation has approved a feasibility study; if the scheme gets the go-ahead, the new centre will have an exhibition area and be used to host events relating to the Great Fire.

Continue up Fish Street Hill and turn right at the junction into Eastcheap. Walk about 100 m (330 ft) and look across to:

33–35 EASTCHEAP [**8**]

This five-floor, highly decorated, Gothic Victorian building was designed by Robert Louis Roumieu in the late 1860s as a vinegar warehouse. With its pointed gables, decorative motifs and carved heads, it is generally considered as having one of the Square Mile's most unique 19th-century commercial frontages. The warehouse was built on or near the site of the former Boar's Head tavern, made famous by William Shakespeare in his *Henry IV* plays as the watering hole of Sir John Falstaff.

Look carefully at the building's facade and above the central window you

33–35 Eastcheap, a former vinegar warehouse

will see a motif of a boar crashing through undergrowth. This is the way Roumieu immortalised the building's history and ensured that the tavern's name lived on.

At the time the vinegar warehouse was constructed, Eastcheap was known for its commercial businesses; however, during the Middle Ages it had been the site of a major meat market when butchers' stalls lined both sides of the street. Like Cheapside (its counterpart further west), it formed part of the processional route from the Tower of London to Westminster.

To the left of the vinegar warehouse you will see Philpot Lane; walk down it. The main entrance to the Sky Garden is on your right, before you reach Fenchurch Street.

20 FENCHURCH STREET [**9**]

Affectionately known as the **Walkie Talkie** and completed in 2014, 20 Fenchurch Street was the brainchild of Uruguayan architect Rafael Viñoly. Uniquely, the 155 m (508 ft) tower has its greatest floorplate at its summit and thus appears somewhat bulky – some say ungainly – from the street. In the course of its construction, its concave design was found to reflect a large amount of sunlight, which damaged

The Walkie Talkie in the City

cars parked in the street. So intense was the beam of light that a City reporter was even able to fry an egg in a pan at pavement level. To prevent the reflection of light, a permanent 'brise-soleil' sunshade was fitted over the glass windows and this seems to have solved the problem.

Inside the Walkie Talkie, an express lift takes you to the large viewing gallery on the 35th floor. Here, you get a fabulous view of the city – either by looking out through the floor-to-ceiling glass walls or from the outside terrace. Floors 36 and 37 are reached via two side staircases and are home to a wonderful landscaped park – the Sky Garden – which is the highest public garden in London. Here you will also find the Walkie Talkie's two restaurants: the Fenchurch and Darwin Brasserie.

There is free public access to the Sky Garden and viewing gallery but you need to order tickets online (www.skygarden.london). As it is very popular, you should book well in advance – be prepared to wait a few weeks for a slot to become available at busy times of the year. The building has recently been sold to the Hong Kong-based company Lee Kum Kee for a record £1.28 billion, the highest amount ever paid in the United Kingdom for a single office building.

Walk to the junction of Philpot Lane and Fenchurch Street. Almost directly across the road is the turning into Lime Street. Walk up Lime Street and turn left at the bend into Lime Street Passage, which leads into the market.

LEADENHALL MARKET [10]

The current purpose-built building dates from the 1880s and was designed by Sir Horace Jones (1819–1887), the 'City Architect' between 1864 and 1887. He used the most popular materials of the day – wrought iron and glass – to construct Leadenhall Market and set it out almost as a series of attached streets beneath a common glass roof. This accounts for Leadenhall's many entrances (on

Leadenhall Market

Gracechurch Street, Leadenhall Place, Whittington Avenue, Bull's Head Passage and Lime Street Passage) and makes it easy to access from the surrounding area.

The market's internal decoration is full of Victorian splendour, with its central brightly painted lantern surrounded by red-and-cream cast-iron Ionic columns. Above today's row of shops you see butchers' hooks that were used long ago when the building was mainly a poultry market. City of London dragons adorn the market, appearing above the main entrances and on the interior columns, while the Corporation's coat of arms is clearly seen on the bollards beside each street entrance.

Take the Leadenhall Place exit from the market and the Lloyd's Building is on your left. At the junction ahead, turn left into Lime Street. Stop in front of the building's entrance.

THE LLOYD'S BUILDING [ı ı]

No one would have believed that such a revolutionary building design would be sanctioned in the somewhat conservative Square Mile of the 1980s, yet Richard Rogers' concept fulfilled the mandate given by Lloyd's for a truly flexible building that would be able to serve the company's needs well into the future.

Rogers maximised internal space by placing all the services and maintenance equipment – pipework, ducts, lifts, air conditioning and power – on the exterior of the building, a technique he had already successfully employed with Renzo Piano at the Centre Pompidou in Paris in the 1970s. In using such an innovative method, he was able to ensure that the building's main room, the Underwriting Hall, could be left totally uncluttered and provide a space able to accommodate up to 10,000 people.

Using stainless steel, glass and concrete, Rogers delivered an entirely novel structure that made Lloyd's stand out from all the surrounding buildings. Despite being overshadowed by lofty office towers in recent years, Lloyd's Building is still totally unique on its site and remains as awe-inspiring now as it was when it was first built over 30 years ago. As it is such an exceptional example of high-tech architecture, it is unsurprising that it attained Grade I listed status in 2011. However, this achievement has its drawbacks, as it means that the very basis upon which the building was designed – its flexibility and adaptability – is now somewhat ironically subject to listed building regulations.

Lloyd's Building

Now turn around and facing you is:

THE WILLIS BUILDING [12]

At 125 m (410 ft) in height, the Willis Building is two and a half times the height of Nelson's Column and taller than its nearest neighbour, the Lloyd's Building. Designed by Foster + Partners and completed in 2008 using a graceful stepped design, the building has three sections – the tallest is 28 storeys high, while the shortest is only six storeys high. Its modern, glass, curved exterior incorporates high-efficiency double-glazing and acts as a wonderful mirror to the Lloyd's Building opposite.

In its design, Foster + Partners took great care to ensure that the Willis Building not only met but also exceeded green expectations. As a result, the building has achieved the highest rating score for its environmental impact, which is achieved by less than 20 per cent of newly completed buildings.

Continue walking down Lime Street towards its junction with Leadenhall Street. The building on the right-hand corner is known as The Scalpel.

The Willis Building

52 LIME STREET [13]

At the time of writing, this highly distinctive building is nearing completion and is due to open in late 2017 as the European headquarters for insurance company W.R. Berkley Corporation. **The Scalpel**, as its name suggests, has sharp angular features in complete contrast to the more curvy Willis and Lloyd's buildings nearby; however, it is more in keeping with 122 Leadenhall Street, which it faces. Taller than neighbouring office towers, it looks set to dominate the EC3 skyline for the near future.

At street level, architects Kohn Pedersen Fox are creating a new public square, a major feature of which is a coffee shop thus ensuring that the City's 17th-century coffee house culture is perpetuated and never forgotten.

Right across the street and slightly to the left you will see:

THE LEADENHALL BUILDING [14]

Known as the **Cheesegrater** because of its tapering triangular shape, this building completed in 2014 is purposely angled at 10 degrees to protect views of St Paul's Cathedral. With 46 levels of office accommodation, it is presently the second-tallest tower in the City of London and is let mainly to financial and insurance organisations. Almost all of the building's services are contained within a separate structure on the north side that is easily identifiable due to its mustard yellow steel framework and red and blue glass, a common feature found in the designs of architects Rogers Stirk Harbour + Partners.

In the early part of 2017, the Cheesegrater was reported to have been sold to a Chinese property mogul for £1.15 billion, slightly less than the Walkie Talkie but still one of the largest Chinese property acquisitions in the United Kingdom to date.

To the right of the Cheesegrater is the site of the proposed new building:

30 St Mary Axe

1 UNDERSHAFT [15]

Planning permission has recently been granted for what will be not only the highest peak in the City (73 floors) but also one of Europe's tallest buildings. The designers, Eric Parry Architects, had originally proposed an even greater tower but were compelled to scale down the height, as it could have been a danger to planes coming in to land at London City Airport.

Although 1 Undershaft is basically a fairly plain rectangular design, it will be clad with external cross bracing to give the building extra structural strength. This feature has led to it being given the nickname **The Trellis**.

When the building is complete, it will offer a public viewing gallery at its summit and, in keeping with other newly constructed high-rise towers, provide a public space at its base filled with retail shops, restaurants and cafes.

Cross over Leadenhall Street and walk up St Mary Axe, past the church of St Andrew Undershaft, until you reach the piazza in front of The Gherkin.

30 ST MARY AXE [16]

Better known as **The Gherkin**, 30 St Mary Axe has become one of London's most instantly recognisable landmark buildings.

Built on the former site of the Baltic Exchange (which was badly damaged by an IRA bomb in 1992), the building won the RIBA Stirling Prize on completion in 2004 and is considered to be London's first ecologically constructed building. Foster + Partners' revolutionary design resulted in a low-energy, environmentally friendly building that used much less energy than other more conventional tower blocks around at the time. The building's exterior diagonal bracing was introduced to allow for column-free floor space and this, together with its glazed facade, results in the provision of much natural daylight. Almost 7,500 pieces of glass were used in the structure but, most surprisingly, only one piece is curved – the lens-shaped cap at the very top of the building.

The Gherkin is 180 m (590 ft) tall, tapers towards its summit and has a private club, restaurant and bar on its top three floors (levels 38–40) that offer stunning views of London. The building was sold for £630 million in 2007, which at the time was Britain's most expensive office-building sale. It changed hands again in 2014 when it was sold for £700 million to the Safra Group, under the control of South American billionaire Joseph Safra.

Continue along St Mary Axe and stop at the junction with Bevis Marks. At the time of writing, the Can of Ham is in the midst of construction on the other side of Bevis Marks.

60–70 ST MARY AXE [17]

Foggo Associates have designed an interesting and unusually shaped office development dubbed the **Can of Ham**. It is considerably lower in height (24 storeys) than its immediate neighbours. However, it is marked out by its distinctive form and should complement the group of new office blocks currently being constructed in this part of the Square Mile. Its design is especially acclaimed for its energy-saving features and includes glazed double-wall cladding and shading fins on the curved facades.

Turn left into Camomile Street and cross over Bishopsgate into Wormwood Street. Turn left at the junction with Old Broad Street. London's oldest tower is on the left-hand side of the street.

TOWER 42 [18]

This was the City's first skyscraper and was formerly known as the NatWest Tower. Seen from above, the building appears to bear a resemblance to the bank's logo of three interlocking chevrons, although its architects, Seifert & Partners, have always refuted this.

Since 2004, it has been largely overshadowed by the variety of new towers that have appeared within the City and are in the midst of construction. When 1 Canada Square was completed at Canary Wharf in 1990, Tower 42 lost its status as the tallest building in Britain; however, it remained the City's highest building until the Heron Tower was completed in 2011.

Work began on the 183 m (600 ft) tower in 1970 and it took ten years to complete. It was designed around a concrete core from which the floors are cantilevered, making it strong but also greatly reducing the amount of space available. This meant that its first owners, National Westminster Bank were only able to accommodate their international banking division here.

In 1993, an IRA bomb in nearby Bishopsgate badly damaged the building. This resulted in it being reclad and refurbished by GMW Architects. It was later sold and renamed Tower 42, the total number of its cantilevered floors. Since changing hands, the building is no longer solely used by bankers but is now shared by a variety of City companies, including hedge funds, corporate law firms, securities and investment firms as well as some overseas banks. Its composition is a good example of the multifaceted nature of the financial City of London. Tower 42 today has a Michelin-starred restaurant on its 24th floor and a champagne bar at its peak that offers brilliant views of the City.

Retrace your steps along Old Broad Street and then turn right into Wormwood Street. When you reach Bishopsgate, you will see the Heron Tower almost immediately ahead.

110 BISHOPSGATE [19]

The **Heron Tower**, located close to Liverpool Street station is just on the edge of the City's high-rise cluster, and is presently the tallest building in the financial district at 46 storeys high. It rises to a height of 230 m (755 ft) and that includes a distinctive 28 m (92 ft) communications mast.

Since the building opened in 2011, it has become one of the City's greatest skyline bar and dining venues. Dedicated glass lifts whiz diners up to the summit in a mere 40 seconds. The Heron Tower owes its sleek modern style to architects Kohn Pedersen Fox and it has won awards for its design. Back in 2014, a dispute arose about its name so it is now officially referred to as 110 Bishopsgate.

Turn left up Bishopsgate. Broadgate is located on the left, behind the Bishopsgate Arcade and right beside Liverpool Street Station.

BROADGATE [20]

This 13-hectare (32-acre), largely pedestrianised development is now home to 17 office buildings, including the celebrated Exchange House (1990) and 5 Broadgate (2016). It is characterised by its four landscaped squares, each surrounded by shops and eateries as well as health and fitness clubs. Walk around the estate and enjoy works of art by famous British and international artists, such as Richard Serra (_Fulcrum_, 1987), Fernando Botero (_Broadgate Venus_, 1989), Barry Flanagan (_Leaping Hare on Crescent and Bell_, 1988), Xavier Corbero (_The Broad Family_, 1991) and Jim Dine (_Venus_, 1989). Displayed out in the open, the artworks are made from materials ranging from stone and ceramics to bronze and steel. For more information about the artworks on display, refer to the 'Broadgate Art Trail' available online at www.broadgate.co.uk.

With over 30,000 workers and visitors, Broadgate runs a program of events throughout the year including sports challenges, art classes and, during the summer months, outdoor screenings of blockbuster movies and sporting fixtures such as the annual Wimbledon tennis championships.

Designed by Skidmore, Owings & Merrill (SOM),, the 11-storey Exchange House is quite unique. It was built, to all intents and purposes, as an enormous bridge across the railway tracks leading into Liverpool Street station. It is an excellent example of the coming together of good architectural design and sophisticated engineering techniques and remains one of the development's greatest successes.

More recently, 5 Broadgate has made its mark on the area and is one of the world's largest stainless steel-clad buildings. Home to UBS, the Swiss global financial services company, it is a 13-storey 'groundscaper' and has revitalised the Broadgate development since its construction was completed in 2016. It was designed by internationally renowned Make Architects, a practice that was launched by Ken Shuttleworth in 2004.

The walk concludes here and you will find plenty of places to eat nearby. Liverpool Street station (Circle, Hammersmith & City, Central, Metropolitan, Overground lines and TFL Rail) is a short stroll away.

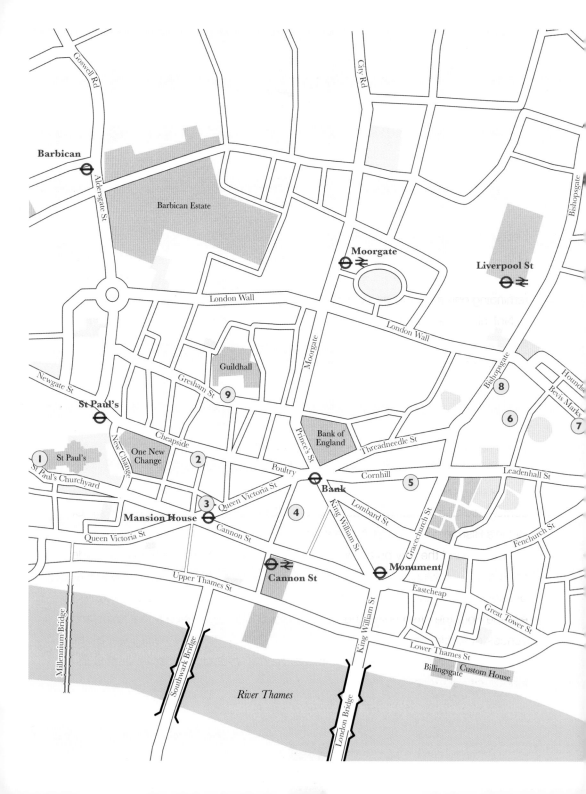

CHAPTER 5

THE RELIGIOUS CITY

Despite the many soaring office blocks that have appeared in the past 40–50 years, church spires are still a remarkable part of the City skyline. Prominent yet graceful steeples, spires and towers poke up amid glass office buildings and skyscrapers, reminding one of a time when the City was home to most of London's population.

Not all of the 87 churches that were destroyed during the 1666 Great Fire of London were rebuilt, and bomb damage during World War II led to a further dwindling of their number, yet still today these religious buildings remain a major feature of the Square Mile, both for their history and for their architecture.

What has changed, though, is how and when the buildings are used. Some now open only at certain times and days, while others share their premises with churches of different faiths (for example, St Dunstan-in-the-West provides services to both the Anglican and Romanian communities). Some churches offer new facilities (for example, a coffee shop in the entrance to St Mary Aldermary), conference and exhibition spaces or even bible study centres (for example, St Helen's Bishopsgate and St Andrew Undershaft).

Walk around the City on any weekday and you are sure to notice signs outside churches publicising free lunchtime concerts – perhaps an organ or piano recital, or even choral singing. These are quite unique events and offer an excellent escape from the often noisy and bustling urban city. Information about times and venues of all church events can be found in 'City Events', the newssheet of the Friends of the City Churches, available at the City Information Centre or at www. london-city-churches.org.uk.

Although the great majority of City churches are Anglican, there are some (such as St Magnus the Martyr) that have a more traditional approach and hold services of Mass and Holy Communion. St Mary Moorfields is the only Roman Catholic church in the Square Mile, while St George's German Lutheran Church is just east of the City boundary in the nearby borough of Tower Hamlets. Austin Friars, close to Old Broad Street, is home to the Dutch church (renowned for its stained-glass windows) and the more recently formed Church of Scientology is based in Queen Victoria Street, beside Blackfriars station.

Jewish prayers are held daily at the Spanish & Portuguese Sephardi synagogue in Bevis Marks, while Islamic services take place in a number of venues around the City. Although there are no mosques within the Square Mile itself, you will find the Brick Lane Jamme Masjid just outside the boundary.

The walk that follows includes only a brief selection of the City's churches and other religious buildings but aims to give you an insight into some of the amazing architectural and historical features of each.

Start the walk at St Paul's underground station (Central line). Immediately in front of you is St Paul's Cathedral. Either walk through the gardens or alongside the railings until you reach the main cathedral entrance.

ST PAUL'S CATHEDRAL [1]

There has been a cathedral here since the 7th century; the present structure is the 5th on the site and was completed in 1711. The earlier churches were subjected to fire and Viking attacks and were replaced at the end of the 11th century by an enormous Gothic building. This cathedral, begun by Bishop Maurice (chaplain to William of Normandy), was even larger than St Paul's is today and was renowned for its exceptionally tall spire and pointed Gothic arches. A lightning strike in 1561

St Paul's Cathedral

brought down the spire, and the cathedral fell into disrepair during the chaos caused by the Civil War in the mid-17th century.

Further serious damage to the cathedral occurred in 1666 as a result of the Great Fire of London. Architect Christopher Wren, as Surveyor of the King's Works, was given the responsibility to design a new cathedral and construction began in 1675. Some 35 years later, having seen five monarchs come and go, Wren completed the cathedral –producing a somewhat different design to that which had been agreed upon when he started. The finished product boasted not just a dome (which had previously been considered too Catholic in style and not in keeping with London's first new Anglican cathedral), but one that was second only in size to St Peter's Basilica in Rome.

Wren built the cathedral in the classical/English baroque style, with tall Corinthian columns and a magnificent pediment above the main entrance. On either side of the pediment, bells were hung within the two towers.

When you stand facing the main entrance to St Paul's, look down on the pavement close to the steps to see the floor plaque commemorating Queen Victoria's Diamond Jubilee in 1897. She was 78 years old at the time and so infirm that the ceremony actually took place outside the cathedral, beside the steps! A painting of the scene can be viewed within the Guildhall Art Gallery (*Chapter 11).

Many events have been held here throughout the centuries: royal weddings (Prince Arthur, Henry VIII's elder brother, to Katherine of Aragon in 1511; HRH Prince Charles to Lady Diana Spencer in 1981), the funerals of British heroes and politicians (such as Admiral Horatio Nelson, the Duke of Wellington, Winston Churchill and Baroness Margaret Thatcher) and many Services of Thanksgiving, such as Queen Elizabeth II's Silver, Golden and Diamond Jubilees.

During World War II, the area was under heavy bombardment yet the cathedral remained standing – it became a symbol of hope for the country. Incendiary bombs fell on the roof but St Paul's Watch, the volunteer force set up to protect the cathedral, dealt with them resulting in minimal overall damage. The much larger bomb that landed outside the south-west tower was removed speedily, saving not only the cathedral but also a great number of lives. To celebrate its 300th Anniversary in 2011, St Paul's Cathedral underwent a major restoration program – so today both the exterior and interior are in very fine order.

Walk up the front stairs and enter the cathedral through the doors on the left-hand side. Tickets are purchased at the booth.

THE NAVE

There is a wonderful feeling of space when you enter St Paul's and it certainly has a far less cluttered interior than London's other famous church, Westminster Abbey. The view looking down the nave towards the dome is quite breathtaking and the cathedral's high ceiling, lack of fixed pews and clear windows contribute to the feeling of light; this is something for which Wren's City church designs are renowned. Although monuments were introduced into the cathedral in the early 19th century, it was not until the late 1800s that Wren's original light-filled building saw the addition of more colour and ornamentation. Queen Victoria had expressed the feeling that the interior of St Paul's was 'dull, dreary and undevotional' and this prompted the introduction of vivid mosaics both on the chancel ceiling and on the arches beneath the dome.

Inside St Paul's Cathedral

The west end of the cathedral, where the visit begins, is dominated by some huge pillars and the great 9 m (30 ft) tall oak and lime wood entrance doors. These are used solely for ceremonial occasions, such as royal weddings, jubilee celebrations, funerals or services of remembrance. Walk down the long central aisle of the nave and, between the arches of the nave and north aisle, you will see the rather unusual and striking monument of the Duke of Wellington (1769–1852) surmounted by his trusted horse, Copenhagen. The memorial was not unveiled until some 60 years after the Duke's death as Church authorities were loath to allow it in the cathedral.

To the left of Wellington's monument and forming an altarpiece in the Middlesex Chapel is William Holman Hunt's superb painting *The Light of the World* (c.1900). It illustrates the figure of Christ knocking on a door that opens from the inside, suggesting that God can only enter our lives if we invite him.

CATHEDRAL DECORATION AND CRAFTSMEN

Wren gathered together a group of highly skilled and talented craftsmen to work with him to build and decorate the cathedral. These included noted woodcarver Grinling Gibbons, French ironworker Jean Tijou, master masons Thomas and Edward Strong, sculptor Caius Gabriel Cibber and decorative painter James Thornhill (the father-in-law of William Hogarth). The excellence and beauty of their work can still be seen in the organ casing, pews, iron gates, carving and stone work within the nave and chancel areas. The original Grand Organ supplied by German organ builder Bernard Smith remained in use until the 1870s, when a new organ by Henry 'Father' Willis replaced it. At this time, Wren's original organ casing was divided in half and placed on either side of the quire, beside the pillars. Remarkably, the casing sections remain largely intact today.

THE DOME

Weighing approximately 66,000 tonnes (65,000 tons) and supported on eight piers, the dome's span is second only to that of the dome at St Peter's Basilica in Rome. Sit in the pews beneath it and wonder at James Thornhill's very fine interior dome painting, *The Life of St Paul*, which is painted in grisaille (monochrome) and appears relatively subdued. Wren had wanted to use mosaics here but this was considered too costly and too foreign. As there was little money available at the end of the building work, he agreed to have a painting solely in shades of grey.

At the base of the painting you will see the Whispering Gallery surrounded by Tijou's black iron railings. It gets its name from the fact that a whisper made on one side of the gallery will be easily heard on the other side, which is really strange! If you are good with heights, climb the 257 steps to the gallery aisle and experience this for yourself.

The dome is considered by many to be Wren's magnum opus but it is not wholly as it appears. Look carefully up into its space and discover the mastery of its construction – the dome we are peering into is actually one of two, an inner and outer dome, separated by a brick cone, giving the strength and support needed for the lantern above.

Beneath the dome in the cathedral crossing, eight very beautiful mosaics adorn the area between the pillars. The work of artists G.F. Watts, Alfred Stevens and W.E.F. Britten, they were gifts from the Grocers, Goldsmiths, Mercers and Merchant Taylors livery companies and were added in the late 19th century. Below them, inscribed on the floor, is a moving epitaph to Sir Christopher Wren (written in Latin by his son) that finishes, 'Lector, si monumentum requiris, circumspice' (Reader, if you seek his monument, look around you).

THE HIGH ALTAR AND AMERICAN CHAPEL

Due to bomb damage at the east end of the cathedral in 1940, the previous Victorian altar was removed and a new altar was installed during the postwar restoration. With a marble base and elaborate canopy (based on an early sketch by Wren) – and surmounted by a figure of Christ in Majesty – the present High Altar is truly magnificent. It was built as both an altar and a memorial to more than 330,000 soldiers from the Commonwealth who lost their lives during the two world wars.

The American Chapel lies behind the High Altar and is endowed with colour in its stained-glass windows. Opened in 1958 in the presence of Vice-President Richard Nixon and Queen Elizabeth II, the chapel reflects the gratitude felt by the British people for America's support during World War II. It is dedicated to the 28,000 Americans who were killed while stationed in the United Kingdom or on their way here during the war; there is a book of remembrance with their names in a glass cabinet.

As you would expect, there are a number of American connections within the chapel. For instance, you see the emblems of each of the 50 US states featured on the windows, Dwight D. Eisenhower's head is carved in wood at the end of the pew benches (as he was the American President when the idea of the chapel was conceived) and the dates 1607 (when the first colony was founded at Jamestown) and 1776 (the signing of the Declaration of Independence) are found on the altar rail. Within the metalwork and woodwork there are also illustrations of the flora and fauna of North America. More subtly disguised in the woodcarving is a rocket, commemorating the role of the United States in space exploration.

THE CRYPT

A walk around the crypt is a fascinating way to find out about British history, its musicians, artists, scientists and naval and military heroes. There are tombs, gravestones, wall and floor plaques plus memorials commemorating the wars and conflicts in which Britain has been involved over the past 300 years. This is where you will find the modest tomb of Sir Christopher Wren – but you might easily pass it by, as it is an unadorned black marble slab and almost hidden from view. On the wall above it, look out for an abridged Latin version of the epitaph that appears on the floor beneath the dome.

Just beside Wren's tomb is a cluster of memorials and graves belonging to famous artists: Anthony van Dyck, Sir Joshua Reynolds, John Singer Sargent, Sir John Everett Millais and composer Sir Hubert Parry. Alongside these is the OBE Chapel dedicated to the honour known as the Most Excellent Order of the British Empire. Created in 1917 by King George V to reward those men and women who had made an outstanding contribution to the World War I war effort, the honour is conferred by the sovereign twice a year on people from all walks of life, ranging from dinner ladies to movie stars. Many athletes, rock stars, singers, musicians, actors, charity workers and even politicians have received the honour during the past 100 years.

Walk towards the rear of the pews and pass by wall plaques on the right remembering those who have made a significant contribution in the field of medicine and science. Ahead you see railings behind which is the imposing tomb of Arthur Wellesley, 1st **Duke of Wellington**. He was a very effective and popular military leader renowned for defeating Napoleon at the Battle of Waterloo in 1815. A real national hero, he was especially celebrated for never having lost a battle. When he died in 1852, more than 8,000 mourners attended his funeral service in the cathedral and the streets were packed with thousands of people who had come to pay their last respects.

On leaving the military, he went into politics and became Prime Minister twice (in 1828 and briefly in 1834). He was Constable of the Tower of London for over 25 years where he was much praised for his overseeing of the site's restoration and the draining of the moat. His name is often mentioned in connection with 'Beef Wellington' and 'Wellington boots', and he is remembered too for phrases such as 'Publish and be damned' (replying to a blackmail threat) and 'The Battle of Waterloo was won on the playing fields of Eton'.

Another major hero, **Admiral Horatio Nelson**, has his tomb nearby, located immediately below the cathedral dome. Having been hit by a French sniper, Nelson died in 1805 on his flagship HMS *Victory* but he lived long enough to know that his strategy had worked and he had managed to defeat Napoleon at the Battle of Trafalgar. His body was returned to England in a barrel full of alcohol and then laid in state at Greenwich in the Painted Hall before his funeral within St Paul's. Nelson, like Wellington, was an extremely popular commanding officer and once again the cathedral was crammed full with his men and many mourners. After the state funeral, his body was placed in the ornate black marble sarcophagus that had originally been made for Cardinal Thomas Wolsey (Henry VIII's Lord Chancellor) in the 16th century. Nelson's viscount coronet, however, replaced the original flamboyant cardinal's hat that Wolsey had designed for his tomb.

In this part of the crypt there are many memorials of more recent skirmishes and battles as well as the tombs of several famous naval and military leaders of the 20th century. There are also monuments and plaques commemorating Americans: a bust of George Washington and a wall memorial commemorating the death of William Meade Lindsley Fiske III, an American pilot who voluntarily joined the Royal Air Force but died in 1940 before the United States entered World War II.

If you are keen to learn more about the cathedral's 1,400 years of history, you might want to visit *Oculus: an eye into St Paul's*, a film experience based in the cathedral's former treasury. Once you leave the crypt, you will find a cafe, toilet facilities and a well-stocked shop. For more formal dining, there is an excellent restaurant close to the cathedral exit.

Walk upstairs to the exit and turn right. At the north-eastern end of the cathedral gardens, cross the main road into Cheapside and walk along the right-hand side of the road. In a few minutes you will arrive at a paved courtyard adjacent to the church of St Mary-le-Bow.

ST MARY-LE-BOW [2]

There has been a church on this site for around 1,000 years. Always one of the City's most important churches, it still retains its 11th-century crypt built of Caen

St Mary-le-Bow church

stone, similar to that used in the Tower of London. Interestingly, its unusual name 'le-Bow' has nothing to do with an archer's bow but relates to the stone Norman arches (bows) in the undercroft area.

Even if you have never visited the church, you might be familiar with its name as it features in the children's nursery rhyme 'Oranges and Lemons'. It was also where a curfew bell rang daily (between the 15th and 19th centuries) at 9 p.m. Traditionally, it is said that a true cockney must be been born within earshot of Bow bells; unsurprisingly, recent experiments have indicated that the bells can no longer be heard as far away as they could in the past due to the noise of London's traffic.

The church of St Mary-le-Bow was badly damaged in the Great Fire of 1666 and was subsequently rebuilt by Sir Christopher Wren, who gave it its much-admired tower and steeple (said to have cost almost as much as the entire church). The main body of the church was destroyed once again during World War II and later rebuilt in Wren's baroque style. Miraculously, his splendid square tower and steeple were left unscathed. Stand on the north side of Cheapside or in the courtyard beside the church to wonder at their beauty and Wren's genius; you can also see the impressive 3 m (10 ft) long copper dragon weathervane, high above the street.

The interior of St Mary-le-Bow is impressive too. Nowadays, it is no longer strictly in Wren's style since new furnishings and vivid stained-glass windows were added in the post-World War II restoration. You can visit this beautiful Grade I-listed church throughout the working week and attend regular daily services. The church does not open on weekends, however, when most businesses are closed and the population of the Square Mile greatly diminishes.

Exit the church and turn right on Cheapside. Take the next right turn, Bow Lane, and cross over Watling Street. You will see St Mary Aldermary on the left.

ST MARY ALDERMARY [3]

St Mary Aldermary (meaning 'Older Mary' to differentiate it perhaps from St Mary-le-Bow) is another church that was rebuilt after the Great Fire of 1666. It is in the Gothic style and possesses a very fine tower. Although attributed to Sir Christopher Wren, doubt exists as to whether he was the architect responsible for St Mary Aldermary, as the church's lengthy nave and aisles do not adhere to his usual classical style.

Inside, the most striking feature is the plaster ceiling with its saucer domes and exquisite fan vaulting (the work of Henry Doogood). Despite 19th-century alterations, the font, poor box and pulpit (possibly attributable to Grinling Gibbons) all date from the 17th century.

St Mary Aldermary is remarkably peaceful even though it is located at a very busy road junction. In its entrance there is a much-appreciated coffee shop with comfy sofas and chairs that acts as a rival to the many coffee houses nearby. It opens weekdays only between 7.15 a.m. and 4.45 p.m.

Exit the church and turn left onto Queen Victoria Street. Turn right just before Mansion House into Walbrook. The church of St Stephen Walbrook is on the left.

ST STEPHEN WALBROOK [4]

This is surely one of the Square Mile's hidden treasures and demonstrates Sir Christopher Wren's genius in design. Walk up the church's entrance staircase, pass through the wood-panelled porch and enter the nave. Then take a few moments to feast your eyes on the space in front of you. Rectangular and in perfect proportion, it is simply like no other church in the City's confines. Wonderfully bright on account of light entering through its lantern, windows and clerestory, there is a feeling of space and loftiness, enhanced by the spectacular

St Stephen Walbrook church

central dome adorned with intricate carvings. Additionally, the rows of Corinthian columns surrounding the dome, the panelled walls and 17th-century woodcarving of the reredos, pulpit, and organ case add to the church's splendour.

The original box pews disappeared in Victorian times and seating is now on contemporary wooden benches. These are set around a somewhat unconventional yet beautifully crafted, circular, travertine marble altar positioned immediately beneath the dome. Henry Moore, the much-acclaimed 20th-century sculptor, was commissioned to carry out the work by Lord Palumbo, the former chairman of the Arts Council, as part of the restoration of the church in the 1970s. He sculpted the altar at the very quarry used by Michelangelo more than 450 years ago! In creating such an altar, Moore hoped to allow congregants and visitors to gather round it, providing a place where God could be found at the centre.

From the moment it was unveiled, the altar – sometimes referred to as 'the big cheese' or 'the camembert' – became the subject of debate and ultimately an ecclesiastical court case was held to decide whether or not it was acceptable as an altar for the Church of England. The highest court of the land resolved the matter and the altar was given leave to remain in situ.

THIS IS THE TELEPHONE
MANSION HOUSE 9000
Found by Chad Varah in the Rector's study,
ready to become the world's first "hotline"
for suidicidal and despairing people,
on 2nd November 1953.
It is the first of many thousands
of emergency telephones throughout the world.
In central London, The Samaritans,
who moved to Soho in 1987,
attend many lines on 439 2224

In the early 1950s, the rector of St Stephen Walbrook, **Dr Chad Varah**, founded the **Samaritans** organisation in order to provide a telephone helpline for despairing and suicidal people. The original telephone used by the organisation can still be seen on display on the west wall of the church. All around

Original Samaritan's telephone

the walls you find memorials and monuments to people associated with the church, including Dr Nathaniel Hodges, who stayed in the City during the Great Plague in 1665 to help those afflicted by lancing boils and providing remedies. Surprisingly, there is no memorial to playwright and architect **Sir John Vanbrugh**, who lies buried in a vault under the church floor.

Since it was built in the 1670s, the church has been considered one of Wren's masterpieces and it is generally thought that he built it as a practice run for St Paul's Cathedral. Wren lived close by in Walbrook and this was his parish church – no doubt he had a special interest in ensuring it was beautifully designed.

Return to Bank junction and walk along Cornhill. Stop outside:

ST MICHAEL'S CORNHILL [5]

You cannot fail to be impressed by the entrance porch and the bronze statue of St Michael placed immediately in front of the church. Magnificently crafted, the tympanum carving above the doorway (by John Birnie Philip) portrays St Michael disputing with Satan and is a fitting entrance into St Michael's Cornhill. Although a medieval parish church existed here from the 12th century, the present church largely dates from the late 17th century and many of its furnishings are even newer, on account of restoration in the 19th century carried out by eminent architect Sir George Gilbert Scott.

St Michael's Cornhill has been famous for its musical tradition since 1375, when it supported a choir of boys, priests and laymen. A 2-manual Renatus Harris organ was built for the church in the 1680s and many notable organists have had the pleasure of playing the instrument in the past 300 years or so, including Obadiah

St Michael's Cornhill

Shuttleworth, William Boyce, Theodore Aylward and Harold Darke (during which time he composed the Christmas carol *In the Bleak Midwinter*). Jonathan Rennert has been the Director of Music and organist at St Michael's Cornhill since 1979.

You may be fortunate enough to hear him play if you drop by the church on a Monday lunchtime when the weekly organ recital is held.

The Drapers' Company has been patron of the church since 1503 and is responsible for its care. Today, St Michael's Cornhill is designated a Grade I-listed church on account of its architecture and features. The 17th-century font where the poet Thomas Gray (who wrote *Elegy Written in a Country Churchyard*) was baptised is still in use and the church boasts some very colourful, 19th-century, Clayton and Bell stained-glass windows. Also dating from the 19th century are the skylights cut in the aisle vaults through which light streams into the church. Despite the darkness of the carved wood box pews, the church feels bright and airy as it is decorated in white, blue and gold, and it is a delightful haven within the City.

Continue along Cornhill and cross the junction with Gracechurch Street into Leadenhall Street. On reaching the Lloyd's Building cross the road and turn into St Mary Axe (the church of St Andrew Undershaft is on the right-hand corner). Walk along the street and, when you reach The Gherkin, turn left into Undershaft. The church is immediately ahead.

ST HELEN'S BISHOPSGATE [6]

Also known as Great St Helen's on account of its size, the church contains an array of impressive wall monuments and magnificent table tombs of affluent 16th-century residents of the area. Sometimes dubbed the 'Westminster Abbey of the City,' the double-fronted church was constructed before the 16th-century Reformation and is extremely

St Helen's Bishopsgate

spacious inside. Unusually, it contains two parallel naves – one is part of a former parish church, while the other is from a Benedictine nunnery that was built beside it. Most of the nunnery buildings have long since disappeared but between the two churches there is an arcade bearing arches from the 14th and 15th centuries, at the south end there is an interesting nun's chapel and on the north wall a louvred opening that permitted the nuns to watch Mass at the altar.

Medieval brasses still adorn the floor and the woodcarving of the pulpit is a wonderful example of Jacobean craftsmanship. Throughout St Helen's you will see some very grand tombs to merchants, liverymen and even mayors. One of particular interest is that of **Sir Thomas Gresham** and it bears his familiar grasshopper crest. (*Chapter 11 has more about the life of this great philanthropist).

Return to St Mary Axe, walk past The Gherkin and take the 2nd turning on the right into Bevis Marks. Walk about 30 m (100 ft) and stop outside the black iron gates of:

BEVIS MARKS SYNAGOGUE [7]

This religious building is unique in being the only synagogue still based in the Square Mile. Regular services have been conducted here since 1701, when the synagogue, built by Quaker Joseph Avis, first opened. It is a Sephardi synagogue whose original members came from Spain and Portugal. Towards the end of the 19th century, Ashkenazi Jews from Eastern Europe and Russia moved into the area and it is their descendants who make up the majority of the Jewish community living in London and the United Kingdom today.

Throughout the early decades of the 20th century, the area was home to many synagogues reflecting the numbers of Jews living and working in the City and East End. Bomb destruction of many of the district's buildings during World War II followed by congregants moving to London's suburbs resulted in Bevis Marks becoming the token synagogue of the area – ultimately representing Anglo-Jewry. Nowadays, the synagogue is often the venue for state and ceremonial services. Commemorations of notable anniversaries, such as VE Day and the start of World War I, have taken place here along with special services honouring leaders such as Sir Winston Churchill and the celebration of an appointment of a Jewish Lord Mayor of London.

Although the synagogue appears quite plain from its façade, the interior contains many wonderful features. Some say that Bevis Marks has the look of a Wren church, with large clear windows, dark oak benches and a gallery above. As it was built in the aftermath of the 1666 Great Fire, when Wren was supervising the reconstruction and restoration of London's churches, his influence upon the design of the building would not be unduly surprising. But probably of greater influence on its decoration was the synagogue in Amsterdam built two decades earlier (where the largest Jewish congregation in Europe was based at the time).

The synagogue's rich interior contains much symbolism: the twelve marble pillars supporting the gallery represent the twelve tribes of Israel, the ten brass candlesticks signify the Ten Commandments, the seven candelabra relate to the seven days of the week and the central chandelier represents the Sabbath. It is also endowed with a very beautiful wood-carved and richly painted Ark.

In addition to daily services, the synagogue is an attractive venue for concerts and weddings (it is famous for its romantic candlelit atmosphere) and its reputation has led it to become a tourist attraction. For details of opening hours, admission fees and tours, refer to www.sephardi.org.uk.

Return to Bevis Marks and turn left, crossing over St Mary Axe and into Camomile Street. Turn left at the junction with Bishopsgate and a few moments later you will reach:

ST ETHELBURGA'S CENTRE FOR RECONCILIATION AND PEACE [8]

This tiny 14th-century church is one of the oldest of the City churches and suffered almost complete destruction by an IRA bomb in 1993. Dedicated to St Ethelburga-the-Virgin, sister to the 4th Bishop of London, Erconwald, the building is one of the few City churches to have survived both the Great Fire and the Blitz.

St Ethelburga's Centre for Reconciliation and Peace

Its fate appeared sealed when the church collapsed in the IRA bombing campaign but reconstruction went ahead and the church authorities decided to reopen St Ethelburga's as a Centre for Reconciliation and Peace.

Today, you find the church wedged in between towering office blocks on a busy main street close to the Heron Tower and Liverpool Street station. Its narrow doorway, tower and turret are dwarfed by the surrounding buildings, yet there is an amazing sense of utter peace inside this light and airy church. Most of the furnishings are modern, with only the southern arcade and 18th-century font remaining from the original church.

Behind the main building, there is a garden set in an attractive Andalusian courtyard with mosaic floor tiles, dominated by what looks like a Bedouin tent. The tent is woven from goat's hair and is a circular space with floor rugs, lanterns and cushioned seating where people gather to talk, conduct workshops and have meetings. It is a wonderful tranquil setting and contains stained-glass windows depicting the word 'peace' written in a variety of different languages.

On its website, the church describes its mission as follows: 'St Ethelburga's is a "maker of peacemakers." We inspire and equip people from all backgrounds to become peace-builders in their own lives and communities.' In order to do this, it offers a regular program of events including talks, communication seminars, discussions and concerts. St Ethelburga's opens daily and encourages the use of the church and garden, both of which can by hired out to groups and organisations.

Exit the church and turn left into Bishopsgate. Cross the road and take the 1st turning on the right, Threadneedle Street. On reaching Bartholomew Lane (beside the Bank of England), turn right and then left into Lothbury. Continue along the street and turn right into Guildhall Yard. Turn left and the entrance to St Lawrence Jewry faces the modern Guildhall buildings.

ST LAWRENCE JEWRY [9]

Standing in Guildhall Yard, right in the heart of the Square Mile, St Lawrence Jewry is the official church of the Corporation of London. It is dedicated to St Lawrence, who was burned alive on a gridiron in the 3rd century ad, and this is remembered in the shape of the weathervane above the spire. The church is so-called because it is situated close by to Old Jewry the street that housed the Jewish population from the 11th century to the 13th century.

St Lawrence Jewry

The medieval church was re-built by Sir Christopher Wren in the 1670s following the Great Fire when it was destroyed. In fact, at almost £12,000 it was probably his most expensive church and is still regarded by many to be the greatest of his churches built in the classical style. Although his building originally sported plain windows (as Wren strived to bring as much natural light as possible into his churches), these were all replaced some 200 years later by stained-glass windows in many designs and by a variety of artists, in keeping with Victorian fashion.

In December 1940, the church was severely damaged due to enemy bombing. Re-construction took place in the late 1950s, this time by Cecil Brown. He painstakingly returned the church to its former glory, adding the imposing chandeliers, a stunningly ornate white and gold leaf moulded plaster ceiling, and employed Christopher Webb to replace the Victorian stained-glass windows. Today, the windows are once again in the style of Wren, although now they benefit from a colourful central panel that not only complements the

Interior of St Lawrence Jewry

colour of the interior decoration but also brings overall lightness into the body of the church.

St Lawrence Jewry is nowadays a guild church, where services relating to the Lord Mayor and Corporation are held. It is greatly associated with the City's livery companies, which have donated much of the church's furniture and furnishings. Alongside the main body of the church, behind a richly decorated wooden screen with winged angels, is the Commonwealth Chapel, where a service takes place every February celebrating New Zealand's national day.

The church is particularly famous for its organ and music program; each Monday and Tuesday lunchtime, piano and organ recitals are held at 1 p.m. In addition, regular evening concerts take place here and the church hosts an annual summer music festival. With such beautiful surroundings and excellent acoustics, it is a favourite haunt of many Londoners.

The tour of the Religious City ends here at Gresham Street, which is about halfway between St Paul's underground station (Central line) and Bank underground station (Central, Circle, District, Northern, Waterloo & City, and the DLR lines).

CHAPTER 6

FILMING IN THE SQUARE MILE

With its splendid buildings, landmarks and pageantry, it is no wonder that the Square Mile appears in numerous movies, television productions and adverts. Old and new architecture sits side by side and there is a maze of Dickensian alleys and courtyards, making this compact area an ideal place to shoot both period and contemporary films. It also has the added bonus of being fairly empty on weekends, when most offices are closed.

Although much filming takes place out on the street, many of the City's institutions, churches, gardens and livery halls appear on film too, with some venues masquerading as other familiar London sites. For example, the Goldsmiths' Hall stood in for Buckingham Palace in the film *Evita* (1996) and more recently in the Netflix series *The Crown*. To the north of the City, Liverpool Street station and Broadgate have been used in a number of television adverts (Converse, Carling, Wella and T-Mobile), as well as for television series such as *Spooks*.

The aim of the following walk is to take you to some of the exciting locations where films have been shot in recent years. It is far from a complete list but it should highlight the range of movies that have been set here and take you to places that you may recognise from the screen. Nearly every day of the year you will find film crews on the City's streets, so keep your eyes open as you wander around – who knows, you might even spot a well-known celebrity!

Start this walk outside Blackfriars underground station (Circle and District lines), on the north bank of the River Thames.

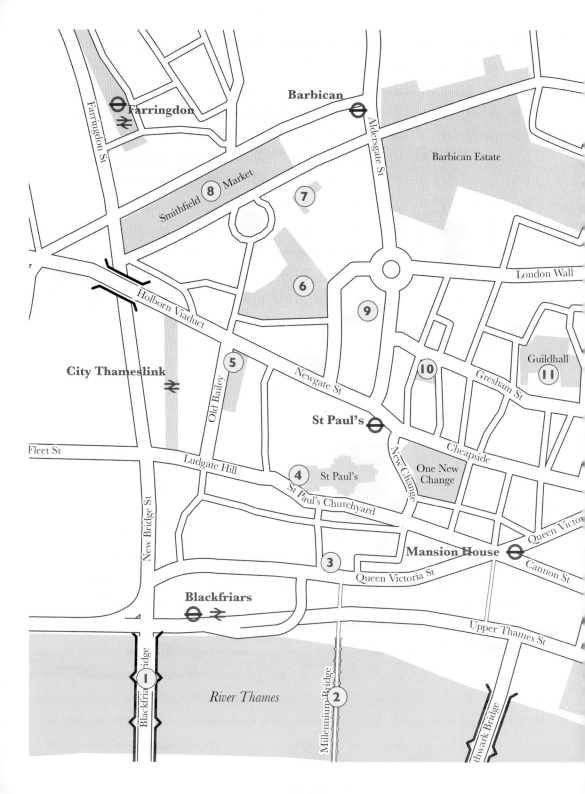

BLACKFRIARS BRIDGE [1]

In his final movie (released after his premature death in 2008), Heath Ledger starred in Terry Gilliam's fantasy, *The Imaginarium of Doctor Parnassus* (2009). It was under Blackfriars Bridge that Ledger's character, Tony, was found hanging – similar to a real-life event that occurred in June 1982. This was when Roberto Calvi, chairman of the Italian Banco Ambrosiano, was discovered by a passer-by dangling from scaffolding beneath the bridge. Initially his death was thought to be suicide. It was later shown to be murder but the killer has never been caught. The press dubbed Calvi 'God's Banker' due to his close association with the Vatican, and certainly he had links with the Mafia as well as other dubious institutions. Despite many investigations, the manner of his death has always been a matter of conjecture.

Cross over Blackfriars Bridge and at the southern end take the stairs down to the riverside. Turn left and walk beside the Thames until you reach:

MILLENNIUM BRIDGE [2]

This pedestrian bridge was designed by Norman Foster, one of the United Kingdom's leading architects, and it opened just before the Millennium in 2000. However, the new bridge was put out of action within days when it was found that the weight of people walking across it made it sway. Unsurprisingly, it was immediately nicknamed the 'Wobbly Bridge' – and it is a name that it retains to this day!

The Millennium Bridge is in fact a suspension bridge that links the area between St Paul's Cathedral on the north bank with Tate Modern, the Globe Theatre and the Southbank arts and cultural centres. It is such a major landmark today that it appears in a great many films. The Bollywood film *I See You* (2006) has a wonderful dance sequence that takes place on the bridge and Harry Potter fans

The Millennium Bridge

will recognise it as the bridge that is destroyed in the opening sequence of *Harry Potter and the Half-Blood Prince* (2009).

Walk across the bridge to the north side of the Thames and continue to Queen Victoria Street. Cross over the road and turn left. In front of you is:

THE COLLEGE OF ARMS [3]

A listed building, the College of Arms has been home to heraldic, ceremonial and genealogical records for 500 years and has been located on Queen Victoria Street since 1555. Today, as in the past, the officers of the College act as genealogical researchers, assisting visitors to find out about their ancestry. In the James Bond film *On Her Majesty's Secret Service* (1969), Bond uses the College to research his rival Blofeld's lineage in the hope of finding his Achilles heel.

More recently, in 2009 the exterior of the building was used as Sir Thomas Rotheram's home in Guy Ritchie's *Sherlock Holmes* starring Robert Downey Jnr and Jude Law.

The College of Arms

To the right of the College of Arms is Peter's Hill. Walk up it, turn left at its junction with St Paul's Churchyard and continue until you reach the crossing. Cross over the road on to the foreground of the cathedral.

ST PAUL'S CATHEDRAL [4]

A very popular backdrop, the cathedral has featured in numerous movie productions. In 2016, it provided the location for one of the main action scenes of *London Has Fallen*, when the American President was under fire from terrorists (the film boasted a star-studded cast, including Gerard Butler, Aaron Eckhart and Morgan Freeman). The final scenes of the 1994 movie *The Madness of King George* (starring Nigel Hawthorne, Helen Mirren and Rupert Graves) were filmed on the cathedral steps; the cathedral also appeared in the opening sequence of *Lawrence of Arabia* (1962) as the venue for T.E. Lawrence's memorial service.

Turn west from the cathedral and walk along Ludgate Hill. Turn right into Old Bailey. Walk along the street until you reach the main entrance of the Central Criminal Court on the right.

THE OLD BAILEY [5]

Not far from St Paul's Cathedral you will see the dome of the Central Criminal Court, better known as the Old Bailey. It is one of several buildings that house the Crown Court and has been the scene of many famous trials throughout its long history. (*Chapter 7).

Naturally, it is a major location for legal dramas. The television series *Law & Order: UK* regularly features scenes based in and around the Grand Hall. Other programs filmed here include *Garrow's Law*, a period drama about the life of 18th-century barrister William Garrow, and the 2013 television legal thriller *The Escape Artist* starring David Tennant and Sophie Okonedo.

Most recently, the court featured in the Benedict Cumberbatch and Martin Freeman television series *Sherlock* (2011–14). However, in both this production and Billy Wilder's film *Witness for the Prosecution* (1957), re-created interior sets of the building were used. Rob Marshall's *Pirates of the Caribbean: On Stranger*

The Old Bailey

Tides (2011) also portrays the court, with Captain Jack Sparrow (Johnny Depp) taking part in an action-filled chase around the Old Bailey and Middle Temple in Georgian London.

If you look up above the main building towards the roof, you see the famous bronze *Statue of Justice*, holding the sword of retribution and scales of justice. This figure appeared in the 2005 film *V for Vendetta*, when the entire building was blown up.

Continue walking along Old Bailey. On reaching the junction at Newgate Street, cross the street and walk directly ahead into Giltspur Street. About 100 m (330 ft) on the right is the main entrance to the hospital.

ST BARTHOLOMEW'S HOSPITAL [6]

Established in 1123 by Rahere, a courtier of King Henry I, the hospital (known as Bart's) is still based on its original site and is one of the City's most respected and internationally renowned medical centres. Today it is regarded as a hospital of excellence, especially for cancer treatment, fertility problems and heart conditions.

In *Bridget Jones: The Edge of Reason* (2004), Bridget steps out of a taxi at the Royal Courts, where she plans to visit her barrister boyfriend, and a passing vehicle drives through a puddle and completely soaks her clothing. This scene was actually filmed outside the Henry VIII gate at St Bartholomew's Hospital.

Entrance to St Bartholomew's Hospital

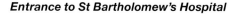

Continue in the same direction; you are now on West Smithfield. Just before you reach Cloth Fair, you will see a small half-timbered gateway ahead of you. This leads to the church.

ST BARTHOLOMEW THE GREAT [7]

St Bartholomew the Great church

Like St Bartholomew's Hospital, a church has existed on the site since 1123. With a stunning Norman interior, it is one of the most impressive churches in the City and a favourite with filmmakers. The fourth wedding in the film *Four Weddings and a Funeral* (1994) took place here and the church has starred in a number of other movies too: *Robin Hood: Prince of Thieves* (1991), *Shakespeare in Love*

St Bartholomew the Great church

(1998), *Amazing Grace* (2006), *Elizabeth: The Golden Age* (2007), *The Other Boleyn Girl* (2008), and Guy Ritchie's *Sherlock Holmes* (2009), *Snow White and the Huntsman* (2012) and *Muppets Most Wanted* (2014). In 2011, it was used by T-Mobile as a stand-in for Westminster Abbey in its *Royal Wedding* advertisement.

Exit the church via the entranceway and turn right. Smithfield Market is straight ahead.

SMITHFIELD MARKET AND WEST SMITHFIELD [8]

During the Middle Ages, this vast space was a grassy 'smooth field' just beyond London Wall and close to the River Fleet. It was an area used for jousting, as a livestock market, for the annual Bartholomew Fair and for large public meetings. In 1305, Scottish patriot William Wallace was executed here (a plaque commemorating him hangs on the wall of St Bartholomew's Hospital). Between the 14th century and the 17th century, Smithfield was the site of many bloody religious and political executions, especially during the tumultuous Tudor period.

Smithfield Market

Its association with blood and gore finally disappeared in the mid-19th century, when the live-meat market moved out of the area and a handsome new building was constructed to house a more hygienic 'dead' meat market. Still going strong, the market operates out of the same buildings, which are now over 150 years old! What has changed, however, are the interior facilities; they are all very modern, in line with the times.

Smithfield is unusual in that it is the only wholesale market to remain in the centre of town. There has been frequent talk of its removal to a less central location in common with Billingsgate Fish Market, Spitalfields and Covent Garden. It will be interesting to see how the site will be redeveloped if and when this takes place.

Unsurprisingly, the highly colourful and ornate Victorian market buildings have always been popular with moviemakers. The creators of the 2009 fantasy thriller *Dorian Gray* (starring Ben Barnes and Colin Firth) elected to use the market exterior to represent King's Cross station.

In the 23rd Bond film, *Skyfall* (2012), West Smithfield became the Intelligence Services emergency HQ following an attack on its premises south of the Thames at Vauxhall Cross. *Last Orders* (2001), starring Bob Hoskins, Helen Mirren and Michael Caine, was also set in Smithfield, with Caine appropriately taking the role of a butcher.

Now, turn left back towards the church. Pass by the entrance and walk down Little Britain and, at the road junction, turn right into King Edward Street. Cross over and turn left through the gateway into:

POSTMAN'S PARK [9]

A delightful green space wedged between St Botolph's, Aldersgate and the former General Post Office buildings, Postman's Park is almost a secret enclave. It is beautifully laid out and even boasts its own somewhat quirky memorial cloister (*Chapter 3).

The 2004 film *Closer* tells the story of four strangers – played by Julia Roberts, Jude Law, Natalie Portman and Clive Owen – and portrays their accidental meetings and relationships. Poignant and full of humour, the movie scene filmed in Postman's Park is where Alice (Natalie Portman) and Dan (Jude Law) fall in love.

Exit the park on the far side and turn right onto St Martin's-le-Grand. Cross the street and take the next turning on the left, Gresham Street. You will see the livery company premises on the right.

THE GOLDSMITHS' COMPANY AND GARDEN [10]

Its sumptuous interiors make The Goldsmiths' Company's premises a filmmaker's delight, especially for period drama and where palatial rooms are sought. The livery company's remarkably ornate Hall is the third to have been built on the site since 1339, when the land was purchased. Designed by architect Philip Hardwick, the Hall certainly demonstrates the wealth of The Goldsmiths' Company; with its highly decorated gold leaf and moulded ceiling, chandeliers (originally candlelit), grand portraits, mirrors and scagliola Corinthian columns, it is really quite magnificent. In addition, there is a Court Room and several wood-panelled rooms, all of which have regularly been used as a backdrop in movies.

With such lavish and opulent furnishings and decoration, it is not surprising that the Hall has doubled as a royal palace in movies such as *Evita* (1996) and *The Lost Prince* (2003) – the story of George V's youngest son, the prince that history forgot – and in the Netflix drama *The Crown* (2016). Other productions that were filmed within the livery company include *Taboo* (2017), *The LEGO Batman Movie* (2017), *The Death of Stalin* (2017), *Woman in Gold* (2015), *Mr Selfridge* (2013) and *Downton Abbey* (2013).

The Goldsmiths' Company has a long history dating back to the trade guilds of the Middle Ages and it is one of the Twelve Great Livery Companies of the City of London. Since the start of the 14th century, it has been responsible for hallmarking precious gold and silver articles, a task that is still carried out in its London Assay Office. Since 1300, it has marked the articles with the King's mark and the leopard's head; this latter symbol can be seen within the livery company's buildings, on its facade and outside at its nearby garden. Today, as in the past, The Goldsmiths' Company aims to foster excellence in jewellery design and craftsmanship, holds exhibitions and programs to support the industry and is involved with its many charitable works and trusts. It is particularly committed to education and provides bursaries to students at UK universities and colleges as well as sponsoring apprenticeships.

Opposite The Goldsmiths' Company premises on Gresham Street, in the grounds of the medieval church of St John Zachary, is its garden, easily identified by the gold leopard heads beside the entrance posts. Scenes from *The Girl with the Dragon Tattoo* (2011) and *Sherlock Holmes: A Game of Shadows* (2011) were filmed within the garden.

Turn right along Gresham Street and walk for about 100 m (330 ft). Guildhall and Guildhall Yard are beside St Lawrence Jewry church.

GUILDHALL [11]

Like the previous stop, the Guildhall (*Chapter 2) has been the setting for a number of acclaimed movies. It was in its cavernous Great Hall that the banqueting scene of *RKO 281* – the 1999 historical drama that chronicled the story behind the making of the classic 1941 film *Citizen Kane* – took place. Scenes from *Mr Bean's Holiday* (2007), starring Rowan Atkinson, were shot in the Guildhall entrance, which was redecorated to resemble a Parisian hotel lobby.

If you are short of time, you have the option to end the walk at this stop. It is a short walk from here to Bank underground station (Central, Northern, Circle, District, Waterloo & City and DLR lines). Alternatively, return to Gresham Street and then turn left into Coleman Street. Walk to the main junction with London Wall and continue straight ahead into Moorgate.

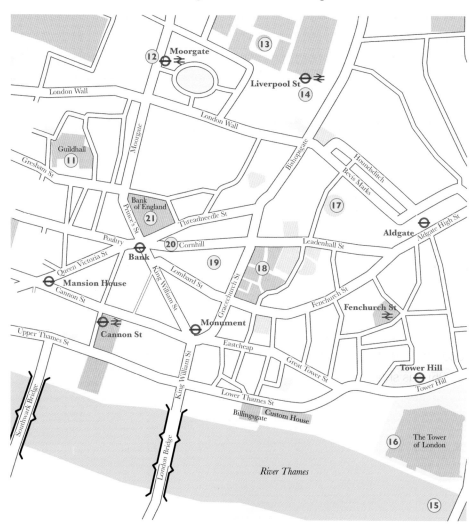

MOORGATE [12]

From Roman times, a small entrance was positioned here in the City wall that was little more than a postern, almost a secret gateway. In the early 1400s, this was replaced with a much more substantial structure and gate that became the last City gate constructed, known as 'Moorgate' and fully part of the City defences. The area just beyond the gate, Moorfields, had always been a large expanse of open moorland and during the medieval period was popular during winter for ice-skating. Following the Great Fire of London in 1666, the land became a refuge for many Londoners who camped out there because their homes in the City had burned down.

Nowadays, Moorgate is where many financial institutions and investment banks are based. It lies to the east of the Barbican Centre and is only a short walk away from the trendy 'villages' of Hoxton and Shoreditch. It is full of interesting buildings and an ideal spot for moviemakers. Two films starring Matt Damon, *Ocean's Thirteen* (2007) and *The Bourne Ultimatum* (2007), were shot in and around the area. In the movie *Batman Begins* (2005), the concourse of the iconic Citypoint building just beside Moorgate and the Barbican Centre is where Bruce Wayne (Christian Bale) unexpectedly comes across Rachel Dawes (Katie Holmes), his childhood sweetheart. The same forecourt appears in *Scoop* (2006) when Woody Allen and Scarlett Johansson are seen tailing Hugh Jackman. Around the corner from Citypoint, at the junction of Moorfields and Moor Place (close to Moorgate underground station), is where a scene from *The Hitchhiker's Guide to the Galaxy* (2005) was shot.

Turn right off Moorgate into South Place and walk straight ahead until it becomes Eldon Street. Broadgate is located to the left of Eldon Street, near its junction with Liverpool Street.

BROADGATE AND BROADGATE CIRCLE [13]

Just 30 years on from its initial construction in the 1980s, Broadgate has transformed what was once the site of Broad Street station and a goods yard into a thriving business centre. Today, advertisers and film production teams regularly use its public spaces and artworks as backdrops in their commercials, adverts and movies.

Spice World, the 1997 Spice Girls movie, was set in Broadgate Circle. More recently, the Broadgate Tower doubled as the Shanghai Building in *Skyfall* (2012) and scenes from *The Counselor* (2013) – with its blockbuster cast of Brad Pitt, Michael Fassbender, Penélope Cruz and Cameron Diaz – were shot in and around the estate. Broadgate also appears in the movies *RED 2* (2013), *Jack Ryan: Shadow Recruit* (2014) and *A Long Way Down* (2014). The estate has also been the setting for a number of television shows, including *The Only Way is Essex,* the crime series *Luther* and the police drama *Above Suspicion*.

Walk down Liverpool Street until you come to the entrance to the station.

LIVERPOOL STREET STATION [14]

One of London's major mainline railway stations, Liverpool Street is another very popular filming location, especially since its modernisation in the late 20th century. It has appeared in a number of books (most famously, H.G. Wells' 1898 novel *The War of the Worlds*), in television series (*Spooks* and *Above Suspicion*) and also in movies. In *The Elephant Man* (1980) this is where John Merrick (John Hurt) arrives in London, and in *Mission: Impossible* (1996) where Ethan Hunt (Tom Cruise) makes a phone call within the brightly lit station.

In 2009, it was the venue for a most unexpected and extremely successful *T-Mobile* advert. Rehearsals took place overnight at the station and it was shot the following morning on the station concourse during the normal working

Kindertransport sculpture

day. Involving more than 300 dancers in commuter clothing, the participants performed a stunning synchronised dance routine. The advert certainly achieved its aim – providing a real element of surprise to everyone in the station. It went viral immediately and subsequently won the television commercial of the year accolade at the 2010 British Television Advertising Awards. The flash-mob advert has since been viewed many hundreds of thousands of times on YouTube.

In the run-up to World War II, Liverpool Street station was where young children fleeing persecution in Nazi Europe first arrived and were welcomed in London. The 'kindertransport' children are today remembered by a couple of particularly poignant sculptures placed around the station. They are the work of sculptor Frank Meisler, who arrived in London on one such train. The largest, showing a group of children with their very few prized belongings, is sited outside the station entrance in Hope Square; another smaller sculpture is close to the underground station entrance within the main station concourse.

Exit the station onto Bishopsgate and walk south until you reach the junction with Camomile Street. Turn left into Camomile Street. Walk the length of the street (it becomes Bevis Marks and then Dukes Place) and continue straight ahead on St Botolph Street. At the junction with Aldgate High Street, turn right and then left into Minories. Tower Bridge looms up in front of you at the end of the road.

TOWER BRIDGE [15]

Naturally, the iconic Tower Bridge has featured in many epic movies. Angelina Jolie is seen riding her motorbike across the bridge in the 2001 movie *Lara Croft: Tomb Raider*; in *The Mummy Returns* (2001), Jonathan (John Hannah) drives a double-decker bus over it. Doctor Parnassus (Christopher Plummer) sets up under the bridge in a corner of St Katherine's Way in *The Imaginarium of Doctor Parnassus* (2009). The opening sequence of *The World Is Not Enough* (1999) and scenes from *Bridget Jones's Diary* (2001), *The Mother* (2003) and *Agent Cody Banks 2: Destination London* (2004) were all filmed here.

In the 2004 movie *Thunderbirds,* the bridge even opened to allow a helicopter to fly beneath it, but possibly the most dramatic sequence ever recorded was in the 1975 film *Brannigan.* A most exciting car chase reached its peak on the bridge as it was opening. In a really thrilling scene, John Wayne's car is seen leaping across the ever-widening gap to safety.

Follow the paths to the piazza in front of the Tower of London.

TOWER OF LONDON [16]

As one of London's most well-known and recognised tourist sites, the Tower has naturally been the setting for an enormous amount of filming and many blockbusters have had scenes shot in and around its precincts.

It would be impossible to mention all the movies that have been filmed here, so the following is just a tiny selection. Most recently, the Tom Cruise and Jeremy Renner film *Mission: Impossible – Rogue Nation* (2015) was shot here, while in 2014 *Muppets Most Wanted* starring Ricky Gervais and Tina Fey included a scene on the Tower ramparts, where Miss Piggy sang a power ballad. A number of *Doctor Who* scenes have been filmed on site as well as Simon Schama's television series *Face of Britain* (2015).

Leave the Tower and cross over the main road, Tower Hill. Turn left and then right into Great Tower Street. Turn immediately right into Mark Lane. Cross over Fenchurch Street into Billiter Street and then turn left into Leadenhall Street. Take the next turning on the right into St Mary Axe and a short way along you come to:

30 ST MARY AXE [17]

Built for the insurance company Swiss Re, the building was immediately dubbed The Gherkin on account of its shape and it is still very much one of the City's signature skyline buildings. In recent years, the trend has been towards creating new towers in this part of the Square Mile, so views of The Gherkin are now sometimes a little obscured. Nonetheless, it is still a popular filming location and has appeared in many recent films. *RED 2* (2013) with Bruce Willis, Helen Mirren and John Malkovich has a fly-by scene next to the building. The Gherkin is where police psychoanalyst, Dr Michael Glass (David Morrissey) has his office in *Basic Instinct 2* (2006) and it also where Chris Wilton (Jonathan Rhys Meyers) works in *Match Point* (2005). The tower appears yet again as the workplace of corrupt market trader Max Skinner (Russell Crowe) in the 2006 comedy *A Good Year.*

Thor: The Dark World (2013) includes a number of scenes shot at The Gherkin, both from within and on the exterior of the building, outside the 36th floor (taken from a cleaning cradle). There is a particularly gripping action sequence that takes place outside on the windows between Malekith (Christopher Eccleston) and Thor (Chris Hemsworth).

Searcys at The Gherkin, housed in the top three floors of the tower, often appears on film as it offers breathtaking views of the capital. It is a private members' club but the restaurant and bar are occasionally open to the public.

Retrace your steps along St Mary Axe and cross over Leadenhall Street. The Scalpel will be on your left and the Lloyd's Building on your right. Continue straight ahead along Lime Street and turn right into Leadenhall Place to reach:

LEADENHALL MARKET [18]

This stunning Victorian market is understandably popular as a filming location. With its splendid architecture and colourful interior, it is a wonderful setting that is full of atmosphere. It's not surprising then that the makers of *Harry Potter and the Philosopher's Stone* (2001) chose the market as the spot to film 'Diagon Alley', the wizarding world's cobblestoned shopping district. In the film, Harry and Hagrid (the half-giant and half-human Keeper of Keys and Grounds at Hogwarts) come here to buy Harry's school wares and this is where Harry discovers the Leaky Cauldron pub for the first time. After visiting Eeylops Owl Emporium Harry buys a snowy owl and calls her Hedwig.

Leadenhall Market has appeared in numerous movies over the years, including *Proof of Life* (2000), *Lara Croft: Tomb Raider* (2001), Clint Eastwood's *Hereafter*

Leadenhall Market

(2010) and *RED 2* (2013). It has also been the backdrop for documentaries, pop and corporate videos, photographic shoots and television dramas.

Exit the market via Gracechurch Street. Turn right and then left at the junction into Cornhill. Walk along until you reach St Michael's Cornhill church, where you turn left into St Michael's Alley. You will see the sign for the Jamaica Wine House on the left.

JAMAICA WINE HOUSE [19]

The Riot Club (2014) was filmed in the Jamaica Wine House (the site of the very first coffee house in the City). Recounting the story of the Bullingdon Club at the University of Oxford, the film follows a couple of first-year students and charts their attempts to join the club. With its wood-panelled interior and partitioned rooms, the Jamaica Wine House is an ideal setting for the dinner scenes in the movie and provides the perfect venue for scheming and conspiracy.

Nowadays, the lovely red-sandstone building is used both as a traditional pub and as a wine bar and it is one of the City's most successful and enduring establishments. It is regularly filled with City workers relaxing at the end of the day, when many of its patrons gather in the quaint alleyway outside. It is interesting to note that locals have been visiting this site since the mid-17th century and then, as now, have always found good conversation, food, hospitality and refreshments here. Back in the late 1600s, when Pasqua Rosee ran his coffee shop on the premises, Samuel Pepys was one of its regular customers and would have no doubt discussed political matters of the day and exchanged City gossip. Over 350 years later, these traditions continue – but be aware that this is strictly a weekday-only venue. If you arrive on the weekend, St Michael's Alley will be a much quieter spot and the doors to the Jamaica Wine House will be closed.

Jamaica Wine House

Return to Cornhill and turn left. Turn right into the alleyway just before you reach the Royal Exchange building.

THE ROYAL EXCHANGE [20]

One of the most romantic scenes in *Bridget Jones's Diary* (2001) was filmed around the back entrance of the Royal Exchange, at its junction with Cornhill, where Bridget (Renée Zellweger) and Mark Darcy (Colin Firth) are seen passionately kissing in the snow. Set at Christmas time, the entire area awash with Christmas decorations and with snow gently falling, Bridget is dressed only in her underclothes, having run out of her flat in search of Mark after he had read her diary.

One of the oldest parts of the City, Cornhill was one of two original hills upon which London was built in Roman times, making it suitable as a settlement. At its western end it joins with five other roads that together make up Bank Junction.

Turn left into Threadneedle Street, where you find the main entrance to the bank.

BANK OF ENGLAND [21]

The Bank of England occupies a sizeable plot of land at Bank Junction and is housed in a most impressive building dating from the 18th century, much of it beneath ground level. (*Chapter 2).

The area around the Bank appeared in the zombie movie *28 Days Later* (2002), when the entire junction was unusually deserted. *National Treasure: Book of Secrets* (2007), on the other hand, was an action movie and staged a thrilling car chase sequence around the area's streets. More recently, Michael Bay's *Transformers: The Last Knight* (2017) carried out shooting in the Bank area.

Bank Junction has been crowded with buses, coaches, taxis, trucks, vans and bicycles, but these were all banished when recent filming took place for the forthcoming production *Mary Poppins Returns* (due out Christmas 2018). The movie, a long-awaited sequel to the original made more than 50 years ago, is set in the 1930s, some 20 years later than *Mary Poppins.* Scenes shot here involved hundreds of extras in period costume alongside vintage cars and an old open-deck bus. The movie boasts an array of well-known actors, with Emily Blunt playing the main role of Mary Poppins; it also includes Colin Firth, Julie Walters, Meryl Streep, Angela Lansbury, Ben Whishaw, Lin-Manuel Miranda and even nonagenarian Dick Van Dyke (who appeared in the original movie).

This is the final stop of the Filming in the Square Mile walk. You will see entrances to Bank underground station (Central, Northern, Circle, District, Waterloo & City and DLR lines) all around Bank Junction.

CHAPTER 7

THE ROYAL AND LEGAL CITY

This walk begins close to the spot that divides the City of London from the City of Westminster, namely the west end of Fleet Street opposite the Royal Courts of Justice. The Courts are not actually within the boundary of the Square Mile but, due to their position on its very western edge, they cannot be ignored in a chapter dedicated to the legal City.

Start the walk outside Temple underground station (Circle, District lines). On leaving the station, turn right towards the Victoria Embankment and then left into Victoria Embankment gardens. Exit at the far end, cross over Temple Place and turn left into a small passageway. Walk up a flight of stairs into Essex Street and at the junction with the Strand turn right. In just a moment you will reach:

ROYAL COURTS OF JUSTICE [1]

The Royal Courts of Justice were designed solely by eminent Victorian architect George Edmund Street (1824–81), and opened by Queen Victoria in 1882, a year after Street's untimely death. Up until this time, there had been a number of courts dealing with civil cases spread across London. Constructing a dedicated court building ensured that all the courts could be accommodated under one roof.

Street's love of Gothic and ecclesiastic styles is immediately evident from the building he designed. With carvings, pointed arches, rose and tracery windows, turrets, spires and towers, the facade of the Royal Courts of Justice looks more

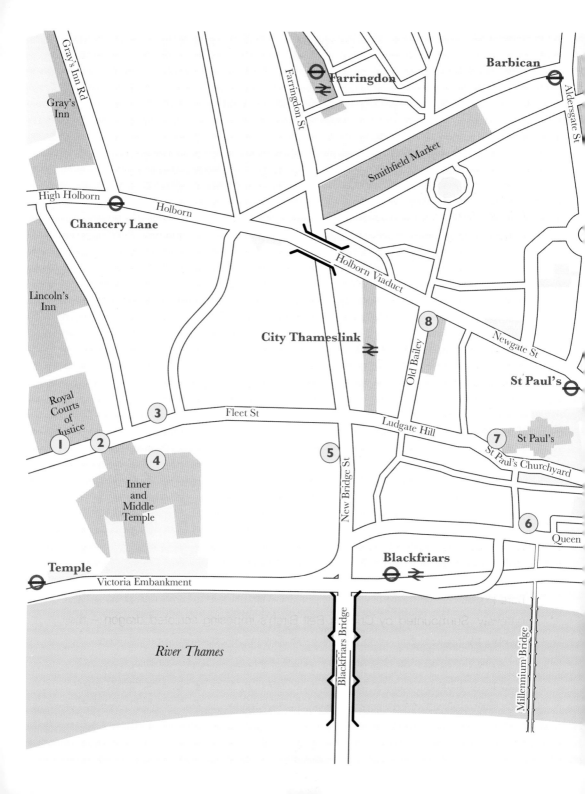

like a church than a public building. The interior too, with its cavernous and lofty hall, is often likened to a cathedral.

Today, the Royal Courts of Justice house the Court of Appeal, which is the second-highest appeal court for England and Wales (the Supreme Court in Parliament Square is the highest appellate court), and the High Court of Justice (with its divisions Queen's Bench, Chancery and Family). On weekdays, members of the public are free to enter the building and generally can sit in the public gallery of any court to watch the trials taking place. The type and variety of cases heard is enormous, ranging from family matters such as divorce and custody arrangements to libel suits, bankruptcy and civil disputes. Many high-profile divorce cases end up here; when they involve celebrities (such as Paul McCartney and Heather Mills in 2008), the street outside is packed full with photographers and journalists jostling to find the best place to stand.

Tours of the Royal Courts of Justice explaining more about the building's history, architecture and artworks are held regularly and can be booked online at www.theroyalcourtsofjustice.com.

Walk along Fleet Street with the Courts on your left, and you will soon see an impressive monument in the centre of the road:

TEMPLE BAR [2]

Although the 17th-century Wren entranceway no longer straddles the street here (*Chapter 10), the present Temple Bar Memorial is a clear marker as a City gateway. Surmounted by Charles Bell Birch's imposing sculpted dragon – the symbol for the City of London – the pedestal features two niches: one containing a statue of Queen Victoria and the other of her son, the Prince of Wales (later Edward VII). They were the last royals to enter the City through the old gate and the event is illustrated on one of the decorative reliefs.

Temple Bar monument

Of all the City entrances, this is surely the most famous as visitors from political Westminster would have had to pass through it in order to reach the Square Mile and trade in the commercial City. Its name, Temple Bar, derives from the area south of where it stands, which is home to Temple Church and is known as the Temple. From the monument, it is only a short distance to the church and two of the legal Inns of Court: Inner and Middle Temple. There are four Inns in total but the other two, Lincoln's Inn and Gray's Inn, are based slightly further north, just outside the City's confines.

Temple Bar has strong associations with royalty, for it is at this spot that the monarch stops before entering the Square Mile and requests permission to enter.

He or she is offered the Lord Mayor's pearl-encrusted Sword of State as a sign of loyalty. During the 2012 Diamond Jubilee celebrations, Queen Elizabeth II and the Duke of Edinburgh took part in a ceremonial procession from Buckingham Palace to St Paul's Cathedral to attend a National Service of Thanksgiving. On reaching Temple Bar, the procession stopped while this very old tradition was enacted. Many watching the television coverage were thus able to see the ceremony for the very first time.

Continue along Fleet Street and stop at:

ST DUNSTAN-IN-THE-WEST [3]

One of two City churches named after St Dunstan (the other one was badly damaged during World War II and is now used as a garden), St Dunstan-in-the-West has two royal associations.

The first appears in a niche over the vestry door: a 17th-century sculpture of Queen Elizabeth I (who reigned 1558–1603) and the only known statue of her to have been carved during her rule. Although she was called the Virgin Queen because she never married, she nonetheless had many suitors throughout her life. Elizabeth claimed that 'I am already bound unto a husband, which is the Kingdom of England'.

Her reign, often referred to as the 'Golden Age', was a time when the country prospered and became a major European power. Elizabeth, in a desire to increase England's position and trade, surrounded herself with daring adventurers – such as Sir Walter Raleigh, Sir Martin Frobisher and Sir Frances Drake – whose maritime and overseas exploits are legendary.

Queen Elizabeth's statue originally stood at the far end of Fleet Street at Ludgate, the City gateway near St Paul's Cathedral, but it was moved here when the gate was demolished for road widening in the latter part of the 18th century.

**Queen Elizabeth I statue at
St Dunstan-in-the-West**

The other royal connection can be seen in one of the windows behind the High Altar. A gift from the local Hoare banking family, the window shows St Anselm and Archbishop Langton with King John at the signing of the Magna Carta in 1215. Known today throughout the world, Magna Carta is possibly the most important document to have been signed by an English monarch, especially as it was forced on the king. It was the most significant of documents drawn up by the barons who were trying to protect their rights and freedoms as well as limit the king's powers by law.

In the many centuries since Magna Carta was drawn up and signed, it has been considered perhaps as Britain's greatest export. Sir Robert Worcester, Chairman of the Magna Carta 800th Committee, has said that 'It is the foundation stone supporting the freedoms enjoyed by hundreds of millions of people today in over one hundred countries'.

After the document was signed, 13 copies were made of it and distributed around the country, many to cathedrals. By so doing, it was impossible for the document to be denied or forgotten at a later time.

Retrace your steps until you are opposite the Royal Courts of Justice. Turn left into Devereux Court, a small passageway leading into Fountain Court and the Middle Temple.

INNS OF COURT [4]

We now enter the Temple area, today an area full of lawyers, but before the 14th century the home to the Knights Templar. This was a religious Order of soldier monks who accompanied and watched over pilgrims on their way to the Holy Land and the London Temple was their headquarters in Britain.

Although initially well respected and supported by the Pope and other rulers, the wealth of the Knights Templar made them the target of obvious enemies and ultimately the Order was abolished in 1312. Their lands were given to an Order of nursing knights, the Knights of the Order of St John of Jerusalem. As these knights already had sufficient lands of their own, they leased the estate to two societies

Middle Temple

of lawyers, Middle and Inner Temple, who were keen to move into the area where they could be close to the royal courts then based at Westminster Hall.

Ever since then, the Temple has been home to lawyers. Each Inn is located in its own campus, not dissimilar to the colleges found at the universities of Oxford and Cambridge. Each campus has its own communal facilities, with a dining hall, chapel, library, gardens and quadrangles as well as chambers, now used as offices but originally used as boarding accommodation for the lawyers.

Both solicitors and barristers are lawyers but, although some of the former carry out advocacy work, barristers more commonly appear in court. Solicitors are usually the people first approached by the general public with legal problems and the solicitors will then consult a barrister to represent their clients in court or to provide them with specialist advice.

Nowadays, would-be barristers at the end of their academic training have to join one of the four Inns of Court for a year's practical training known as 'pupillage'. During this period, prospective barristers are compelled to attend 12 'qualifying sessions' that historically have comprised formal dinners in Hall followed by debates, lectures, recitals or moots.

On qualifying, barristers look to gain 'tenancy' within a set of chambers. About 80 per cent of barristers are self-employed and commonly share premises (chambers) and overhead costs with other barristers but they do not operate as a company or partnership. Each set of chambers employs a Barristers' Clerk to administer and manage their business activities and these clerks will take bookings from solicitors and agree fees on behalf of the barristers.

MIDDLE TEMPLE

Middle Temple is instantly recognisable through its symbol, the lamb with a staff, conspicuously displayed all around the Inn and on its buildings. With its wonderful Elizabethan buildings and atmospheric grounds (cobbled streets, gas lighting and manicured gardens), it is not surprising that the Inn is in demand as a film and television location. Movies such as *Sherlock Homes, The Wolfman, Bridget Jones: The Edge of Reason, Pirates of the Caribbean* and *The Good Shepherd* have all been shot here as well as period dramas and advertisements.

MIDDLE TEMPLE HALL

Built in the Tudor period, Middle Temple Hall has one of the most magnificent double hammer-beam roofs in the country. Throughout its 450-year history, lawyers have debated, undergone training, dined and been entertained in the Hall under

its exquisite roof. It has always been considered a fashionable venue and it is believed that the very first performance of William Shakespeare's *Twelfth Night* was performed here in 1602. Even today – continuing its age-old custom of entertainment – trainee lawyers, barristers and Benchers write and take part in the Christmas Revels that are held annually within the Hall.

In addition to its roof, the Hall is renowned for its exceptionally long 'high table' and the cupboard that stands below it. The former was a gift from Queen Elizabeth I and consists of three planks from a single

Middle Temple Hall

oak tree in Windsor Forest, while the latter is believed to have been made from the hatch cover of Sir Francis Drake's ship, the *Golden Hinde*. Newly qualified barristers, on being called to the Bar, sign their names at this cupboard.

During the week, the Hall opens to the public between 10 a.m. and 12 p.m. and tours of the building can be booked by emailing events@middletemple.org.uk. The Hall and several other period rooms are available for hire and are frequently the venues for weddings, banquets, corporate hospitality and meetings.

Many famous people have associations with Middle Temple. Renowned diarist John Evelyn was a member of the Inn in the 17th century as was Charles Dickens in the 1800s. All US Ambassadors to London become Honorary Benchers; both Her Majesty Queen Elizabeth The Queen Mother and Diana, Princess of Wales were Royal Benchers in their lifetimes. Prince William, Duke of Cambridge is the current Royal Bencher.

Now pass through the archway, cross Middle Temple Lane and walk through Pump Court. Go through the Cloisters into Temple Court.

TEMPLE COURT AND TEMPLE CHURCH

Here in Temple Court you see Temple Church on the north side and **Inner Temple Hall** on the south side. The latter suffered great bomb damage during World War II and was replaced in the postwar period by a much more modern building. Generally, it is closed to the public but you might be able to gain entry during the annual London Open House weekend in September. On a daily basis the Hall, like its counterpart in Middle Temple, is used for dining, functions and events.

The building is easily recognised by its symbol, Pegasus the flying horse, which you will find liberally dotted around Inner Temple's campus on railings, drainpipes, external furniture, above doorways and building frontages.

Temple Church is used as a chapel by both Inner and Middle Temple, with lawyers from the former sitting on the south side and Middle Temple lawyers sitting on the north side. The church dates from the late 12th century and was built in the Gothic style by the Knights Templar. Originally based on the circular Church of the Holy Sepulchre in Jerusalem, Temple Church is divided into two parts: the Round (which is renowned for its wonderful acoustics) and the Chancel. Heraclius, patriarch of Jerusalem consecrated the Round in 1185.

Some 55 years later, Henry III indicated that he intended to be buried in the church, so the early Choir was demolished to make way for a much larger and grander one. Ultimately, the king changed his will and was buried in Westminster Abbey, leaving Temple Church with a particularly ornate interior. Sir Christopher Wren refurbished it after the Great Fire in 1666; in the 1840s, it was restored by the Victorians, who attempted to bring it back to its original appearance (which would have been brightly coloured). Badly damaged during the bombing raids of World War II, the church once again underwent restoration. Subsequently, the Glaziers' Company donated a wonderful new east window that illustrates some of the people associated with the church, including Henry II and Henry III.

Unusually, Temple Church is a Royal Peculiar under the direct jurisdiction of the monarch and is headed by a Master, officially appointed by the sovereign. The church is highly regarded for its musical tradition and holds regular Wednesday lunchtime organ recitals and also offers a concert program. Both the Temple Church choir and the Harrison & Harrison organ are world famous.

Just outside the church in **Temple Court** you see a graceful column with a bronze sculpture of two knights on horseback. The work of artist Nicola Hicks, it reflects an ancient image representing the humble origins of the knights.

Leave Temple Court via the archway, walk across the cobblestones and turn right towards the river onto King's Bench Walk. Walk down to number 11.

11 KING'S BENCH WALK

These were Tony Blair's chambers before he became Prime Minister in 1997. You can see his name inscribed on the door notice board along with that of Lord Irvine of Lairg. The latter became Lord Chancellor in Blair's government but was also known for introducing Blair to his wife when the two were studying to become barristers. Giving a speech at their wedding, Lord Irvine credited himself as 'Cupid QC'.

Walk back up King's Bench Walk to the gatehouse at Tudor Street. Turn right to leave the precincts of Inner Temple and exit via the gate. Walk along Tudor Street until you reach New Bridge Street and turn left.

BRIDEWELL PALACE AND PRISON [5]

We now move away from the lawyers, over to the site of what was once a royal palace occupied by Henry VIII during the early part of his reign. It was an important residence not far from Westminster and was used by the king after Westminster Palace burned down in 1512. Although famous in its day (for it was here that Henry VIII's Lord Chancellor, Cardinal Thomas Wolsey, met with the Papal delegation to discuss the annulment of Henry's marriage to his first wife, Katherine of Aragon), by the reign of his son, Edward VI, the palace had become a home for the poor, an orphanage and a house of correction. It was later used as a poorhouse and a prison. Over its 300 or so years of use, the name 'Bridewell' became synonymous with large institutions, prisons and houses of correction and the term was known not only in Britain and Ireland but also as far away as the United States.

The original palace was large and roomy, consisting of two brick-built courtyards with an inner three-storey high building in which the royal accommodation was located. It covered a substantial area of land, stretching south of present-day St

Bride's Church in Fleet Street to the Thames at the end of New Bridge Street (by the present-day Unilever building opposite Blackfriars station).

Edward VI gave the palace to the City of London in 1553, after which time its original function as a palace all but disappeared. During its use as a poorhouse and house of punishment for disorderly women, and later a prison, the inmates did not have an easy life. Following the custom of the day, it was thought that in order to reform those incarcerated in the prison they should receive punishment and be made to work. Thus, many of the women were given work relating to the wool trade and cloth-making (including spinning, winding silk, carding and knitting) and the male inmates would be involved in ironwork, making nails, working in the mills and unloading sand used in the building trade.

The entire institution was closed in the mid-19th century and demolished some time later. Nothing remains of the original Tudor palace today although a plaque can be seen in St Bride's Place commemorating Bridewell Palace. If you stand outside No 14 New Bridge Street a rebuilt Gatehouse has been incorporated into the office block above and has a relief portrait of its main benefactor, Edward VI on its frontage.

Edward VI's keystone

Cross New Bridge Street at the crossing opposite The Blackfriar pub, turn left and walk along Queen Victoria Street until you reach a red-brick building with elaborate black gates and railings.

COLLEGE OF ARMS [6]

This wonderful Tudor building has existed on this site since the 1600s and is one of the very few buildings from this period still remaining in the City of London. It is an institution that is particularly pertinent to the royal theme of this walk, as the Heralds, who run the organisation, continue to be responsible for great Ceremonies of State, such as Coronations, the State Opening of Parliament and State funerals. In addition, they organise the annual service and procession of the Order of the Garter held at Windsor Castle. While performing these duties, they wear traditional distinctive scarlet uniforms (and tabards) with the Royal Arms embroidered in gold on the sleeves, front and back.

The College (its formal title, The Corporation of the Officers of Arms in Ordinary) was chartered in 1484 by King Richard III. For most of the time since then, Heralds have been members of the Royal Household, appointed by the sovereign following the recommendation of the Chief of the College of Arms, the Duke of Norfolk, Earl Marshal. The Duke's office is hereditary in his family and, as a Great Officer of State, he has responsibilities and special managerial (supervisory) powers over the 13 Heralds and the College of Arms.

Nowadays, it is the duty of the College of Arms to grant new coats of arms and also to keep listings of genealogies, Royal licences, flags, arms and pedigrees. It remains the official heraldic body and has jurisdiction for much of the Commonwealth as well as for England, Wales and Northern Ireland. Members of the public can visit the building on weekdays between 10 a.m. and 4 p.m. and tours of the Record Room are available by special arrangement.

Exit the College of Arms and turn left into Queen Victoria Street. Turn left again into Peter's Hill. Stop opposite the cathedral.

ST PAUL'S CATHEDRAL [7]

St Paul's features in a number of the City walks, probably because it is so intertwined with the life of the Square Mile. Although not the Coronation Church (that is the role of Westminster Abbey), it has had and continues to have many associations with the monarch and royalty.

Prior to the construction of the present cathedral, royal events had occurred here (although infrequently). In 1588, Queen Elizabeth I attended a Thanksgiving Service to celebrate the defeat of the Spanish Armada; such services were conducted over the centuries by other monarchs to acknowledge and honour military victories and peace treaties.

By the 19th century, this had become established practice. When the Prince of Wales recovered from a bout of typhoid, Queen Victoria commanded that

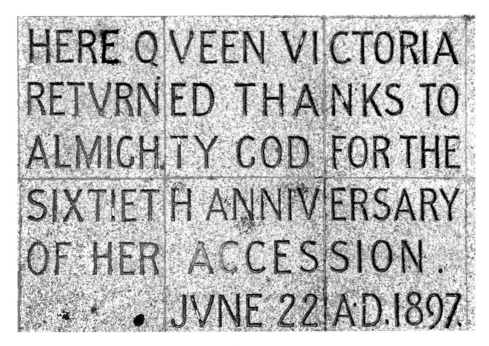

Plaque to Queen Victoria outside St Paul's Cathedral

a Thanksgiving Service be held here to rejoice in his recovery. Some 25 years later, as an old lady, she rejoiced in her Diamond Jubilee outside the west (main) entrance to St Paul's.

In recent years, we have celebrated the Silver, Golden and Diamond Jubilees of our present monarch, Queen Elizabeth II, as well as Services of Thanksgiving to mark both the Queen's 80th and 90th birthdays and her mother's 100th birthday in 2000.

However, the cathedral has rarely been used for royal weddings, with the exception in 1981 of HRH Prince Charles to Lady Diana Spencer. The spectacular fairytale wedding was seen by over 750 million people across the world and many still remember both the magnificence of the occasion and the bride's wedding dress, with its train measuring almost 8 m (26 ft) in length. The only other royal wedding to have been held here was in Old St Paul's in 1501, when Prince Arthur married Katherine of Aragon, a marriage that only lasted six months due to his untimely death.

Turn left, pass by the City Information Centre and then cross over Ludgate Hill at the crossing. Walk down the hill and take the 2nd turn on the right, Old Bailey. Walk the length of the street and stop near the junction with Newgate Street.

THE OLD BAILEY [8]

It seems fitting to end the walk at one of London's – if not the world's – most notorious criminal courts, the Old Bailey. Built on the site of what had been Newgate Prison, the present building dates from 1907 (with a 1970s extension by McMorran & Whitby) and was designed by E.W. Mountford in the neo-baroque style. Its dome proudly stands at 60 m (197 ft) above the street and is surmounted by the impressive gold-leaf figure of Justice with arms outstretched, standing

The Old Bailey

upon a globe and carrying the sword of retribution and scales of justice. Contrary to popular belief, the figure is not blindfolded.

The sculptor, Frederick William Pomeroy RA, also created the statues and inscriptions decorating the building's grand entrance. Above the door, he carved a verse from the Bible – 'Defend the children of the poor and punish the wrongdoer' – and placed allegorical stone statues above the portico. In the middle is the Recording Angel, her head covered in a cowl and writing on a scroll, flanked by Fortitude on the left, carrying a sword for war and a dove for peace, and Truth on the right, looking in to a mirror.

The interior lobbies and magnificent immense staircase in Mountford's courthouse are highly decorated with allegorical paintings, mosaic arches, intricate carvings and Sicilian, Greek, Italian, Belgian and Swedish marble. Originally only four courts were built but over time others have been added and there are now eighteen in total. Here, major criminal cases in Greater London dealing with felonies such as murder, fraud, treason, theft, perjury, rape and arson are heard, although cases involving similarly heinous crimes from elsewhere in England and Wales may be tried in the Central Criminal Court too.

Courts 1 and 2 in the old building are probably the most famous and they are where some of the Old Bailey's most high-profile cases have been tried. Court 1 was where the trial of Soham murderer Ian Huntley took place in 2003, serial killer Yorkshire Ripper, Peter Sutcliffe in 1981 and also the East End gangsters, the Kray twins in 1969. The court has a public gallery but seats are small and there is little legroom, although that has never deterred spectators! Court 2 is used as a high-security court and is where terrorist trials take place.

If you plan to visit the Old Bailey, be warned that there are strict security measures in place: mobile phones, backpacks, penknives, food and drink are not permitted inside the building and no provision is made to leave your belongings there. It is also advisable to carry some form of identification, especially if you intend to sit in on a high-security case. The courts sit on weekdays between 10 a.m. and 1 p.m. and again from 2 p.m. to 4.30 p.m. Before you go, to give you an appreciation of how the justice system worked during the 19th and 20th centuries, you might want to read Charles Dickens' *A Tale of Two Cities* or John Mortimer's *Rumpole of the Bailey*.

We have now reached the end of the Royal & Legal City walk. The nearest underground station is St Paul's (Central line), a short walk east along Newgate Street.

THE LIQUID AND CULINARY CITY

FROM 17TH-CENTURY COFFEE HOUSES TO MODERN-DAY PUBS, BARS, DINING & SKYLINE VENUES

COFFEE HOUSES

Walk around the Square Mile today and you will never go hungry or thirsty! With coffee chains such as Starbucks, Costa, Caffè Nero and Pret A Manger on almost every corner, the coffee shop is booming once again. These coffee 'temples' are not only the place to pick up a drink en route to the workplace but they are also where business is carried out and office workers increasingly conduct small meetings. In fact, the very same practices that took place within the City over 350 years ago!

The first and possibly the best-known coffee house in London opened in St Michael's Alley in 1652. It was run by Pasqua Rosee, manservant to merchant Daniel Edwards, who worked for the Levant Company and traded in Turkish goods. Edwards helped Rosee to set up his business and coffee was sold at his premises for a penny a cup. The coffee house was such a great success that many others followed in its wake – at one time there were said to be as many as 3,000 such establishments. Each coffee house associated itself with different areas of interest, laying the foundations for many of the City's present commodity markets. It was in the coffee houses that merchants met and discussed affairs of the day, establishing contacts and doing business.

Coffee houses appealed to different groups of people perhaps offering a specific service: for instance, you might visit to consult a medical practitioner or to organise publication of a book. A number were frequented by Americans; from around 1730, the New York Coffee House became the centre of intelligence for all connected with US trade, the Pennsylvania catered to shipping interests and the Virginia and Baltic attracted people involved with the American plantations. Edward Lloyd concerned himself with marine matters and Lloyd's coffee house became the hub for shipowners and underwriters from the 1680s.

Today, there is little evidence remaining of these institutions apart from some blue wall plaques along Exchange (now Change) Alley commemorating both Jonathan's and Garraway's that were once sited here. Both were famous in their time. Garraway's had been one of the first to sell tea, was the birthplace of the Sun Fire Office and was frequented by stockjobbers during the South Sea Bubble of 1720. Jonathan's clientele ultimately formed themselves into the Stock Exchange and later moved to their own premises. The coffee houses around Cornhill always attracted bankers, stockbrokers and merchants, while those in the west along Fleet Street were less business focused and appealed more to literary types, actors and men of wit.

In time, as the commodity markets became more and more established within the City, the coffee houses lost their former significance and began to close down. Who knows, perhaps the trend will change once again at some time in the future? But for now, it looks very much as though City coffee shops are here to stay.

SKYLINE BARS AND CITY DINING

With the preponderance of high-rise office buildings, the City now has an increasing number of spectacular skyline bars and dining facilities, many of which are open to the public. Buildings such as **Tower 42**, the **Heron Tower** and the **Walkie Talkie** (20 Fenchurch Street) all have bars on their upper floors as well as separate restaurants, often run by renowned chefs. Although **The Gherkin** (30 St Mary Axe) is generally only open to private members, it has 'open nights' when the bar and restaurant can be booked by the general public too; visit www.searcysatthegherkin.co.uk for the most up-to-date information.

Sadly, **Lloyd's of London** does not offer public dining facilities but you might be lucky enough to gain entrance to the iconic building during the London Open House weekend held in September each year.

Roof Terrace at One New Change

Not as high as the buildings so far mentioned, yet still with stunning views of St Paul's Cathedral and the River Thames, is the roof terrace at **One New Change** at the west end of Cheapside. **Madison** opens daily here from 11 a.m. It has an excellent cocktail bar and a restaurant serving grills, burgers and wraps. In the summer months, a pop-up cinema arrives on the roof and shows movies on the terrace overlooking the cathedral.

A five-minute stroll down Cheapside will bring you to a pink and cream granite building near Bank Junction. This is **No. 1 Poultry**. Take the lift to its French restaurant, brasserie and bar on the roof, **Coq d'Argent**. From the penthouse location you get fabulous views of the Royal Exchange, Bank of England and the City skyline. Almost directly opposite, at the end of Poultry, is the newly opened **Ned Hotel**, named after the building's architect, Sir Edwin 'Ned' Lutyens. Built as the head office of the Midland Bank in the 1920s, the building has just been painstakingly converted by the Soho House group into a magnificent hotel and members' club. The former opulent banking hall is now home to nine different dining areas separated by imposing green stone columns and rows of walnut banking counters. Each restaurant represents a different country or region and offers European, American or Far Eastern cuisine.

Just a little further north from the Ned Hotel, on the edge of the Square Mile, is the **Angler Restaurant**. Located on the 7th floor of South Place Hotel by Finsbury Circus, this Michelin-starred fish restaurant is headed by Executive Chef Gary Foulkes and renowned for its excellent seafood dishes and fresh seasonal fare.

Going east from here brings you to **Broadgate** (beside Liverpool Street station), with its cluster of dining and drinking options. It has an enormous variety of food outlets as well as street and fast food and good fine-dining restaurants. Lovers of oriental food should try out **Shoryu Ramen** (specialising in foods from Japan's southern island, Kyushu) or **Yauatcha City**, which offers contemporary Cantonese dishes and is noted in particular for its superb dim sum range.

Near **Liverpool Street station** you will come across **Jamies Wine Bar**. This is part of a chain of bars owned by Jamie Oliver dotted all around the Square Mile. He also runs a barbecue steakhouse, **Barbecoa**, beside St Paul's Cathedral in One New Change (on the bottom level of the shopping mall), which is famous both for its steaks as well as its enormous range of American whiskies.

Just a short distance from Liverpool Street but outside the City's boundaries is **Spitalfields**, once a thriving fruit and vegetable market but nowadays full of clothing and craft stalls as well as cafes, boutiques, fast-food stalls and restaurants. Beside it in **Spital Square**, in a wonderfully restored 19th-century schoolhouse chapel, is the restaurant, **Galvin la Chapelle** run by the celebrated Galvin brothers. Known for its superb food offerings, it is located in the most charming, grand Grade II-listed building that has been likened to a cathedral. With a Michelin star and an interesting, adventurous menu, the restaurant certainly merits its continued popularity. The à la carte menu does not come cheap but the restaurant does offer a prix fixe lunch menu, early dinner menu and Sunday roast lunch menu that are competitively priced.

A few moments away on the eastern edge of the City is **Brick Lane**. Renowned for its authentic curry houses, Brick Lane is also full of galleries, markets, clubs and bars. **The Old Truman Brewery** is a favourite venue for food, music, shopping and events. Brick Lane and the streets that radiate from it are vibrant, colourful and full of life, especially in the evenings and on weekends.

Back in the Square Mile, there are two popular restaurants in **Devonshire Square** (off Bishopsgate). **Kenza**, specialising in food from Morocco and Lebanon, is located in a luxurious basement decorated in the traditional Middle Eastern style. With its beaded lamps, comfortable satin cushions and tasteful fountains, the restaurant is the ideal place for a celebration. Kenza not only offers great food and a wide range of Lebanese mezes, tagines and teas, but it also entertains its customers with a belly dancing show. In contrast, **Cinnamon Kitchen** provides contemporary Indian dining. Executive chef, **Vivek Singh** is renowned for his creative modern Indian food and runs regular masterclasses introducing customers to his highly successful culinary techniques. Nearby in **Devonshire Row** is **The Bull and The Hide**, a pub and restaurant as well as a small boutique hotel. The restaurant is highly acclaimed for the quality of its food, which uses organically reared meat and fish from London's major food markets, Smithfield and Billingsgate. Food for its vegetarian options is sourced from another of London's famous markets at Spitalfields.

The pub, The Bull, is entered at street level and serves excellent bar meals and snacks. Upstairs in a separate room is The Hide restaurant, where you can sample the chef's modern British cuisine that relies upon fresh seasonal produce. Located close to Liverpool Street and the office blocks on Bishopsgate, The Bull and The Hide is busy throughout the day, mainly frequented by local workers and City visitors.

Closer to Bank junction, along Basinghall Street, is **Hawksmoor Guildhall**, which is renowned for its excellent provision of beef, range of steaks and seafood. Offering hearty breakfasts, à la carte dining and seasonal set menus, it remains one of the Square Mile's favourite business dining options. **Sauterelle** restaurant and the **Grand Café** in the **Royal Exchange** are also popular venues for their beautiful setting and the quality of their food.

Grand Café, Royal Exchange

Other restaurants to look out for are **Sweetings Restaurant** on Queen Victoria Street, near Mansion House underground station, Michelin-starred **Club Gascon** right by Smithfield Market and **Vanilla Black** close to the Royal Courts of Justice in Took's Court. The

Simpson's Tavern

latter is considered to be one of the best vegetarian restaurants in London and aims to 'redefine contemporary non-meat cuisine'.

For a more Dickensian feel, you should visit **Simpson's Tavern** in Ball Court just off Cornhill. Founded in 1757, the tavern claims to the oldest chophouse in London and is a wonderful remnant of times gone by. Still serving breakfasts and lunches that Samuel Pepys and Charles Dickens would recognise, Simpson's Tavern attracts a regular clientele of City workers and visitors who appreciate good traditional English food. Be warned, though – it is only open on weekdays and closes by around 4 p.m.

Alternatively, if you seek a jaw-dropping view of the City, visit **Duck and Waffle** or **SUSHISAMBA** on the top floors (38–41) of the **Heron Tower** (110 Bishopsgate).

Duck and Waffle

Duck and Waffle, occupying the top two floors of the tower, is London's only 24/7 skyline restaurant and opens for breakfast, lunch, dinner and serves meals throughout the night. Its menu is wide and varied, including snacks, small plates, steaks and veggie cuisine. If, however, you prefer Japanese–Brazilian–Peruvian fusion dishes, SUSHISAMBA is the place to go. A visit to either restaurant is exciting at any time of the day but experiencing a sunset or sunrise from the Square Mile's tallest building is something truly memorable.

Another sky-high venue is **Vertigo 42**, the bar and restaurant at the top of **Tower 42**, popular as much for its traditional afternoon tea as for its evening cocktails and fine dining. In Tower 42 you also find Jason Atherton's Michelin-

Sky Garden, 20 Fenchurch Street

starred **City Social** restaurant. Situated on the 24th floor, the restaurant is recognised for its innovative menu, its quality of food, lavish furnishings as well as its breathtaking views.

Close by at the **Walkie Talkie** (36th and 37th floors) are the **Fenchurch Restaurant** and **Darwin Brasserie**. Set among the wonderfully tended greenery of the Sky Garden, both restaurants provide a range of menus as well as à la carte dining. Views from the restaurants look out south across the Thames and never fail to impress!

The Shard, London's tallest building, is located on the south bank of the Thames and is easily spotted from the buildings mentioned earlier. Nearly 310 m (1,020 ft) high, it has viewing terraces on its 68th, 69th and 72nd floors that are almost twice as high as any others in London (www.theviewfromtheshard.com). Like the towers on the north side of the river, this iconic building contains a good selection of bars and restaurants from which you can enjoy fine views of the Square Mile. On a clear day, you can see as far as 65 km (40 miles).

Also along this side of the Thames is **Tate Modern.** Here on the 9th floor of the recently opened Blavatnik Building you can dine at the restaurant looking directly across the Thames to St Paul's Cathedral, especially beautiful at night when it is lit up.

If heights are not your thing, then for a totally different experience why not lunch in the historic **Middle Temple Hall**, home to many of the United Kingdom's lawyers. Here you will sit beneath a magnificent oak hammer-beam roof and dine among barristers and their pupils within an exquisite Elizabethan Hall decorated with coats of arms and wood-panelled walls. Middle Temple Hall opens Monday to Friday in legal term time between 12.30 p.m. and 2 p.m. Lunch consists of three courses and is well priced at £25–30; there is also a bar for light and alcoholic refreshments. It is a popular venue, so you will need to book in advance (events@ middletemple.org.uk). Guests are required to follow Middle Temple's dress code, the details of which are described on its website. To dine in the Hall feels like a real privilege and is made all the more exciting by knowing how many famous people have themselves wined, dined and debated at these very tables since the Hall's construction in 1574.

Another historic venue that provides excellent dining is the **Café Below.** Located at St Mary-le-Bow church on Cheapside, the restaurant occupies the vaulted stone crypt beneath the church. Menus (breakfast and lunch) abound with home-made fresh and seasonal food. The cafe is a wonderful contrast to the busy city above and it is a privilege to be able to dine in such a charming and intimate space.

PUBS AND INNS

You will find all manner of pubs in the Square Mile. Some date back several centuries and have bags of character, while others are newly built and fit well within the style of the modern architecture.

There are far too many to name and thus the following section describes only a tiny selection of what is available. In truth, there is no standard pub in the City – some are wonderfully concealed in narrow courts and alleyways, while others have been converted to their present use from earlier banking halls and coffee houses. **The Viaduct Tavern** beside the Central Criminal Court claims to contain prison cells within its cellar, the beautifully decorated Art Nouveau **Black Friar** was built on the site of a former monastery, and the **Cockpit** on St Andrew's Hill has associations with William Shakespeare, who owned a property nearby.

The Viaduct Tavern

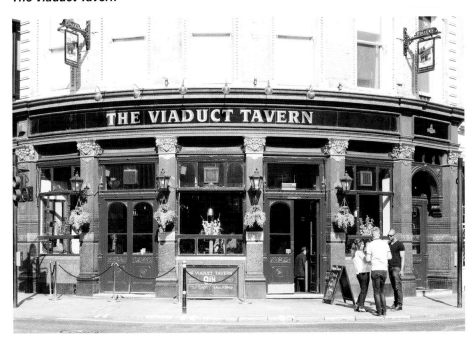

The Cockpit

Certainly, you never have to walk far to find a pub in the City of London and most establishments provide food as well as drink. Some have dedicated restaurants (usually in an upstairs room), some extend into several bars and others provide large screens, particularly popular for sporting events.

As most City offices are shut on Saturday and Sunday, many pubs traditionally close over the weekend – so it is best to check opening times online if you are intending to visit a particular pub. Opening times vary during the week but all pubs tend to close at 11 p.m. unless they are hosting a special event or have extended licensing hours.

Listed below and arranged by area are some of the Square Mile's best-known and loved watering holes:

FLEET STREET AND ENVIRONS

Ye Olde Cheshire Cheese	Dates from the 17th century and is associated with Dr Samuel Johnson, Charles Dickens, Mark Twain, Theodore Roosevelt and other literary giants.
The Tipperary	Supposedly London's first Irish pub, established by Dublin brewer S.G. Mooney & Sons in 1700. It claims to be the first pub outside Ireland to sell Guinness.
The Punch Tavern	Renowned for its elaborately decorated interior and tiled lobby. It was at this pub that *Punch* magazine was purported to have been set up in 1841.
Ye Olde Cock Tavern	With a very narrow frontage, it has been on this site since 1888. Inside it retains some good traditional features, including a flagstone floor.
The Old Bank of England	Dating from the late 1880s, it was formerly the law courts' branch of the Bank of England (beside the Royal Courts of Justice) and its grandeur has not been lost in its conversion from banking hall to public house.

The Old Bell Tavern	Sir Christopher Wren designed the present building in 1670 to accommodate the workers rebuilding (the adjacent) St Bride's Church after the Great Fire. In the 15th century, this was where Wynkyn de Worde (William Caxton's assistant) set up his printing press.
El Vino	During Fleet Street's printing era, this was a popular wine bar and great haunt of journalists and lawyers. Built towards the latter part of the 19th century, its interior bar and dining areas are delightful. Today the bar mainly attracts a business clientele and opens weekdays only.
The Knights Templar	Situated on Chancery Lane, this is another grand bank conversion, now part of the Wetherspoon empire.

SMITHFIELD

The Bishops Finger	Sourcing its meat from the nearby Smithfield Market, this pub is noted for its quality food. It is a typical local pub serving up a wide selection of Shepherd Neame ales and lager.
Butchers Hook & Cleaver	Once a bank, the building had a makeover in the late 1990s and has become a modern Fuller's pub.

Hand and Shears	Despite its fairly plain interior, it is an interesting example of many Victorian pubs in London, containing three distinct bar areas with wood panelling and wooden floorboards.
The Hope	Based in a Grade II-listed building, the Hope serves 100 per cent free-range meat pies that have won awards and it has a dedicated gin parlour upstairs.
Rising Sun	Located in Cloth Fair opposite St Bartholomew the Great church, the pub has all the traits of a local pub and opens all week long.
Fox & Anchor	Decorated in the Art Nouveau style with etched glass and colourful tiles, the Fox & Anchor offers food, drink and rooms. Built at the end of the 19th century, it has a wonderful facade designed by W.J. Neatby, the man responsible for Harrods' food hall. The pub still opens at 7 a.m. on weekdays to cater for the porters working in nearby Smithfield Market.
The Viaduct Tavern	The pub has an excellent position directly opposite the Old Bailey (Central Criminal Court) and is famed for its fabulous interior decoration, in particular the three painted panels on the back wall designed in the Pre-Raphaelite style. Cells from the former Newgate Prison are alleged to exist in the Viaduct's basement and the place is said to be haunted.

BLACKFRIARS AND ENVIRONS

The Blackfriar	Utterly unique, this is one of the City's gems. The pub gets its name from the priors who wore black robes and who lived on the site when it was a 13th-century priory. (You can see a statue of one on the exterior facade.) The Art Nouveau interior is really unexpected, with wall friezes illustrating the antics of the monks. Its vaulted dining area set back from the main bar is adorned with marble and alabaster.
The Cockpit	Hidden away behind busy Queen Victoria Street, this attractive building sits on a corner straddling two streets. It has been the site of a public house for more than 400 years and it is believed that William Shakespeare might have come here in the late 1500s when he purchased a property nearby. For many years, the pub was popular for its cockfights but these stopped long ago. Today, it is a pub full of character and, unusually for the City, it remains open on weekends.

BOW LANE

Williamson's Tavern	This is not an easy pub to find – as it is tucked away in a court off Bow Lane – but it is well worth the effort! While much of the Square Mile is now full of modern developments, this is an area more akin to

Charles Dickens' time. You can almost sense some of his characters walking about the narrow streets and courts and can imagine how the area would have looked when it was gaslit. Williamson's Tavern exists on what was once the formal residence of the Lord Mayor of London. After the Lord Mayor moved in to Mansion House in the mid-18th century, the building became a hotel. It changed direction again in the early 20th century and is now very much a City inn.

BANK AND ENVIRONS

Jamaica Wine House	Located on the site of London's first coffee house, the Jamaica Wine House sits just behind St Michael's Cornhill church in a medieval alleyway off Cornhill. Dating from the late 1800s, the pub has a splendid Grade II-listed wooden interior and extends into several partitioned rooms. It is one of the City's best-known and popular venues, as illustrated by the crowds seen drinking both inside and outside the pub on a summer's evening.
The Counting House & The Crosse Keys	Both establishments began life as vast banking halls and, as such, are extremely ornate. When transformed into drinking halls in the late 1990s, much care was taken by the brewing companies (Fuller's: The Counting House; Wetherspoon: The Crosse Keys) to retain the plush decoration. They certainly stand out

amongst the canon of City pubs, with their elaborate chandeliers, glass-dome skylights, marble, pillars and dark polished wood. They are also both renowned for their selection of ales.

View of Tower 42 from the Duck and Waffle

LEADENHALL MARKET

The Lamb Tavern

Although a tavern existed on the site in 1780, the current building appeared when the present market was constructed in the late 19th century. The Lamb Tavern occupies a prime position within the market and is a marvellous example of Victorian craftsmanship, with etched-glass windows and doors, wooden fittings and a tiled panel showing how Sir Christopher Wren intended to rebuild London after the Great Fire. The pub is particularly frequented by those working in the vicinity and it is common to see well-heeled men and women standing outside the pub with an after-work drink in hand before heading home.

ALDGATE

The Hoop and Grapes

Located on the very edge of the City and dating from the 1590s, this is possibly the Square Mile's most historic inn. It is also the only timber-framed pub that remains in the City today. Remarkably, it survived both the Great Fire of 1666 and the bombing during World War II; it was meticulously restored and renovated during the 1980s. Look closely at its facade and you will see that it leans out – this crookedness seems to give the pub even more charm. The Hoop and Grapes opens every day except Sunday and serves food as well as drink.

BISHOPSGATE AND LIVERPOOL STREET STATION

Dirty Dicks

Dirty Dicks acquired its somewhat unusual name from a local merchant who, in despair after the untimely death of his fiancée the night before their wedding, refused to ever wash again. From the day his beloved died, he kept all the wedding feast and wedding cake in a locked room. After the merchant's death, the pub landlord bought the wedding paraphernalia and put it on display in the pub. People immediately flocked to see the amazing collection (including some mummified cats) and Dirty Dicks became very successful. Over the years, much of the memorabilia has been thrown away but one small glass case has been retained containing a few of the original artefacts. The pub, full of atmosphere, is still popular; it opens daily and stays open until 3 a.m. from Thursday to Saturday.

Hamilton Hall

Today this is a Wetherspoon public house based beside Liverpool Street station. Built as the Grand Ballroom of the Great Eastern Hotel in the early 20th century, it was from the beginning lavishly decorated with many mirrors, marble, allegorical figures, paintings, chandeliers and high ceilings. The fittings and furnishings have largely been restored and Hamilton Hall remains one of Wetherspoon's most elaborately decorated London branches.

TOWER HILL

The Hung Drawn and Quartered	Taking its name from the hangings and executions that once were common on nearby Tower Hill, the pub is a stone's throw away from the Tower of London. Its traditional food menu specialises in pie and mash, although the kitchen also serves a wide range of other foods (including breakfasts and light lunches). Grim tales about the Tower are found on the walls along with portraits of royal and famous personages.

UNUSUAL VENUES

Naturally, where a good deal of money is made, there is money to be spent and although the West End has been the traditional home for London's entertainment, nowadays much greater emphasis has been put on the supply of culinary excellence and entertainment within and around the Square Mile. In addition to the many restaurants, inns and bars already described, there are some wonderfully quirky entertainment venues – proving that the City is not the stuffy financial centre one might expect.

In recent years, several themed bars have burst onto the scene: **Swingers, located** beside The Gherkin, is a basement decked out with two crazy golf courses, cocktail bars, a gin terrace and deck plus a street-food area. Open daily from midday until late, it's a great place to hang out (but only if you're over 18!). Another great basement venue is **Bounce** in Holborn (adjacent to Chancery Lane station). Its theme is ping-pong but you can also relax at its bar or go for the dining option. Just on the northern City border, by Finsbury Square, is **Flight Club** – noted for its great cocktails and fast-paced darts games using state-of-the-art technology. This is the place to come with a group (maximum 20 players); you will

Swingers

benefit from instant scoring and multiplayer games. Food and drink are served as you play and charges (£15–25) are by the hour.

East of the City, in The Old Truman Brewery, is another crazy golf venue – **Junkyard Golf Club**. You can bring kids here at off-peak times (before 7 p.m. Sunday–Wednesday) and try out four different courses. The place is famed for its loud music, its Junk Food Kiosk and bar.

Recently moved westwards from its Whitechapel base, **Whistle Punks** is the place to visit for an urban axe-throwing experience! Don't worry if you haven't slung an axe before, as staff members are on-hand to train you. Based in a warehouse close to Vauxhall station, it still attracts a City clientele and is within easy reach of the Square Mile.

One last bar to mention here is a seasonal pop-up run by the **London Shuffle Club**. Opening for short periods in the summer and winter months, the club is packed with indoor shuffleboard courts and several table shuffleboards – it is a very social sport. Presently without a permanent home, it moves around various locations, most recently in The Old Truman Brewery in Brick Lane.

Speakeasy bars are also a favourite with City workers. **The Mayor of Scaredy Cat Town** near Liverpool Street is particularly unusual. To gain entry, you must first go to the Breakfast Club on Artillery Lane (close to Liverpool Street) and ask to see 'the Mayor'. This provides the key to entry via the door of a white Smeg fridge, reaching the secret bar at the foot of a staircase. The Mayor of Scaredy Cat Town prides itself on its interesting selection of cocktails, great variety of spirits and international range of beers and ciders; it is a really cosy setting.

The Bootlegger near Leadenhall Market is also inspired by the speakeasy era. The entrance is through a narrow street doorway on Lime Street and the bar itself lies deep underground. Decorated in the style of a 1920s US prohibition bar, it plays live music, serves lavish cocktails and even runs masterclasses to instruct you in the art of mixing your very own cocktails.

The Square Mile also has its own cabaret venue: **Proud Cabaret City.** Close by Fenchurch Street station, in a luxurious underground

Proud Cabaret City

Victorian Bath House

space, it resembles a vintage Hollywood supper club and offers high-end dining and entertainment in the form of burlesque, cabaret, jazz, live bands and shows. Open Thursday to Saturday, this is a place to come and party late into the night.

And finally, if you are passing by Bishopsgate churchyard (beside St Botolph's church), look out for the **Victorian Bath House**. You cannot miss its elaborate tiled and domed exterior, so utterly at odds with its surroundings. Built originally as a suite of underground Turkish baths in the 19th century, it was decorated with stained-glass windows, vivid ceramic tiles, mosaics and marble floors. When the baths closed in the 1950s, the building became a restaurant and later a nightclub. Nowadays, it functions as a cocktail bar on Fridays and hires out its rooms for private events during the week.

MARKETS AND SHOPPING

Throughout history, the citizens of the City of London bought and sold goods at markets and trading in the street was commonplace for hundreds of years. A walk along Cheapside (the Oxford Street of the City in the Middle Ages) confirms the statement above. Have a look at the names of streets that cross its main path. You will come across Bread Street, Honey Street, Poultry, Wood Street and Ironmonger Lane, all a reminder of the produce and goods once sold at these spots. 'Chepe' was the Anglo-Saxon term for 'market' and Cheapside was a central market area. It was close to the River Thames and produce arriving by water could be easily transported here from the quayside.

Over the centuries, specialist markets became established at Smithfield (meat), Leadenhall (meat, poultry and game), Billingsgate (fish) and Spitalfields on the edge of the Square Mile (fruit and vegetables). New buildings were constructed for each market in the latter part of the 19th century and, with the exception of Spitalfields, were designed by Sir Horace Jones (1819–87), Surveyor and Architect to the City from 1864, who also designed Tower Bridge.

Initially, the markets would have traded from stalls and sheds, perhaps operating on only certain days of the week. For example, a Royal Charter for a cattle market at Smithfield was set up in 1636. In 1682, King Charles II granted a Royal Charter to silk thrower John Balch, giving him the right to hold a market on two days a week in or near Spitall Square (the area we now refer to as Spitalfields). At this time, Londoners would regularly go to markets to buy fresh provisions and these places were their main source of goods.

Following the Great Fire of London 1666 and the Industrial Revolution of the 18th and 19th centuries, metropolitan London's population exploded – increasing from 1 million in 1801 to 6½ million by the end of the century. Many new shops selling food, clothing, household goods, furniture and furnishings appeared as people moved into the capital and the newly established suburbs. Within the Square Mile, however, there was a definite decline in population during the same period (from 129,000 down to 27,000), largely on account of the removal of slum properties and their replacement with large and often elaborate commercial buildings. The drop in numbers was even more marked following World War II, when so many of the City's houses, offices and retail outlets were devastated by enemy bombing. Only since the building of the Barbican residences in the 1970s has the population risen from its postwar low of 5,000 to about 8,000 in 2017. The City today has by far the smallest residential population in all the 33 London authorities and yet its daytime population swells dramatically. It is largely because of these numbers that the provision of shops, cafes and restaurants has grown so much in recent times.

No longer is the City a gentleman's enclave, full of men in pinstriped suits, bowler hats and carrying an umbrella. Nowadays, it is full of workers of both sexes, in less formal attire, and shops accommodating their needs have sprung up all across the business district. Department stores **Marks and Spencer** and **House of Fraser** both have a presence here and there are numerous womenswear and menswear shops around Liverpool Street station, Broadgate, in Cheapside, on Bow Lane, Fleet Street, Holborn, Cornhill, Fenchurch Street and Paternoster Square. **The Royal Exchange** has continued with its age-old tradition as a trading venue; now it is very much a centre of luxurious goods (retailers include Aspinal of London, Church's, Hermès, Leica Camera Ltd, Montblanc, Paul Smith, Smythson and Tiffany & Co.). It opens weekdays only and services mainly those employed and making money in the Square Mile. Within its stunning building, there is a variety of wining and dining possibilities ranging from the Threadneedle Bar to the Grand Café in the central courtyard and restaurants Sauterelle and Imperial City.

Coming around full circle, Cheapside has reasserted itself as a major shopping destination with its award-winning shopping mall **One New Change**. Designed by French architect Jean Nouvel, it is full of well-known brand outlets and has an exciting roof terrace, bar and restaurant. The mall, which opens daily, has become extremely popular with both City workers and tourists in the area and it is a great place to shop for clothes.

One New Change

In recent years, local branches of all the main UK supermarkets have appeared in the City, enabling workers to pick up food for lunch or dinner. Although the traditional markets have not entirely disappeared, only Smithfield still sells fresh meat on its site. Billingsgate Market relocated east to Docklands back in 1982 and Leadenhall Market no longer sells fresh poultry and meat (the last butcher, Ashby's, moved out about a decade ago). Leadenhall is now best known for its restaurants, shops and bars. Likewise, Spitalfields fruit and vegetable market has moved out to Leyton and the original marketplace now functions as a consumer market selling clothes, crafts, artworks, food and jewellery.

Increasingly common around the City are the lunchtime markets that offer delicious street food from across the world. They are found in venues such as Guildhall Yard, Fenchurch Street station piazza, Paternoster Square, Leadenhall and Spitalfield Markets where there are always crowds of people queuing to buy good-value meals at the stalls.

The modern financial City has definitely moved with the times. No longer is the West End the only place to shop for clothes and accessories – the City can match it with its superb variety of markets, shops and stores.

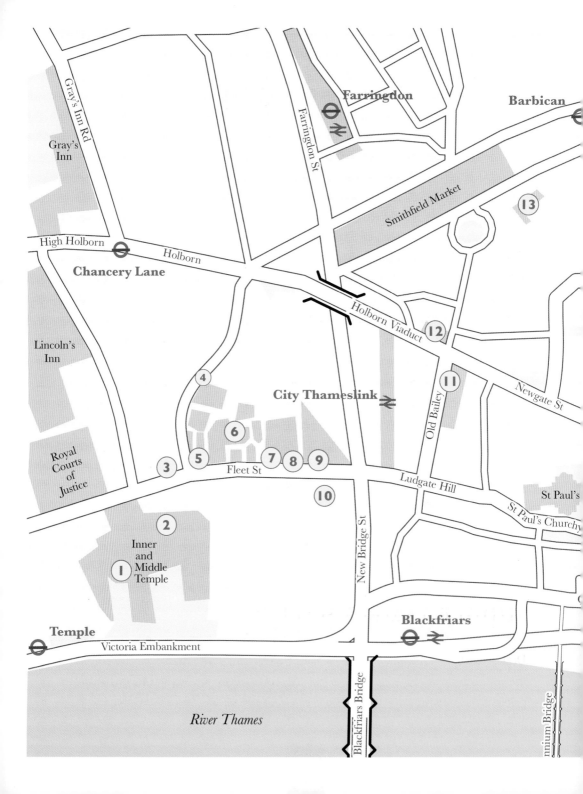

Gray's Inn Rd

Gray's Inn

Farringdon

Farringdon St

Barbican

Smithfield Market

⑬

High Holborn

Holborn

Chancery Lane

Holborn Viaduct

⑫

Lincoln's Inn

④

City Thameslink

⑪

Newgate St

Old Bailey

Royal Courts of Justice

⑥

③ ⑤

Fleet St

⑦ ⑧ ⑨

Ludgate Hill

St Paul's

St Paul's Churchy

⑩

② New Bridge St

Inner and Middle Temple

①

Blackfriars

Temple

Victoria Embankment

Blackfriars Bridge

River Thames

mnium Bridge

CHAPTER 9

THE CITY AND ITS NORTH AMERICAN CONNECTIONS

Start the walk outside Temple underground station (Circle, District lines). On leaving the station, turn right towards the Victoria Embankment and then left into Victoria Embankment gardens.

As you walk through the gardens beside the station, you might be interested to discover that the road and gardens did not exist until the latter part of the 19th century. Before this, the area was part of the River Thames and under water. Only when the Victoria Embankment was constructed was land reclaimed from the river; the gardens were added and landscaped with planting beds, trees and statues.

Exit at the far end of the gardens, cross over Temple Place and turn left into a small passageway. Walk up a flight of stairs into Essex Street and at the junction with the Strand turn right. Take the next right turn off the Strand, pass through Devereux and Fountain Courts and stop beside Middle Temple Hall.

MIDDLE TEMPLE HALL [1]

Middle Temple Hall is greatly associated with two Elizabethan explorers, Sir Francis Drake (c.1540–c.1596) and Sir Walter Raleigh (c.1552–1618), who attended the Inn, not to become advocates but to acquire legal training in preparation for public service. In many ways, the Inns of Court at this time were considered to be

England's third university and it was common for sons of merchants and noblemen to study here to obtain knowledge of the law.

Both the flamboyant adventurers organised and undertook voyages to the New World during the golden Elizabethan age of exploration. When Drake returned to London in 1581, after sailing the globe and founding New Albion (present-day California), he was given a magnificent banquet in Middle Temple Hall. He was once again feted by the Benchers and members after his successful expedition to the New World in 1586.

Exit Fountain Court and cross Middle Temple Lane into Pump Court. Then pass through the cloisters into Temple Court. The church is on the left.

TEMPLE CHURCH [2]

Since 2015, the church has been exhibiting a copy of the 800-year-old Magna Carta, the principles of which Middle Temple members exported to the colonies in the 17th century when they settled in the New World; the principles later became incorporated into the American Bill of Rights and the Constitution. In fact, five members of Inner and Middle Temple signed the Declaration of Independence in 1776.

During the 18th century, a great number of Americans – largely from Virginia and South Carolina – studied at Middle Temple, including seven signatories of the 1787 American Constitution. Links between the two countries have continued since then and today the US Ambassador to London, Chief Justice and Attorney General as well as former presidents of the American Bar Association are all Honorary Benchers of the Inn.

Within the church itself, you will find the effigy of William Marshal, 1st Earl of Pembroke. He famously acted as mediator between King John and the barons in 1215 and was one of the king's advisers at Runnymede who managed to secure the agreement embodied in Magna Carta. The Earl later became guardian to the boy king, Henry III, after the death of King John. Magna Carta was reissued in 1216 and 1217 under the Earl's seal, ensuring its continued existence, and again by Henry III in 1225. The Earl's son, another William, later married Henry III's sister and is buried in the church close to his father.

A more recent American connection involves composer Hans Florian Zimmer, who recorded part of the film score for the 2014 movie *Interstellar* within Temple Church. Zimmer, who lives in California, is head of the film music division at DreamWorks Studios and is renowned for integrating electronic music sounds with traditional orchestral arrangements. He has composed more than 150 film scores, including *The Lion King* (1994), the *Pirates of the Caribbean* series and *Gladiator* (2000).

Exit Temple Court through the archway onto the cobbled stone square and turn left into Old Mitre Court Buildings. At the end of the passage, cross over Fleet Street and turn left. Walk a few paces until you see the church on your right.

ST DUNSTAN-IN-THE-WEST [3]

Established about 1,000 years ago, the church has been on its present site for nearly 190 years. Today, it is not only an Anglican City church but it also provides regular services to the Romanian Orthodox Church. Renowned for its links to North America, the church boasts a memorial to **George Calvert, 1st Baron Baltimore** (c.1578–1632), who is recognised as the founder of Maryland.

Calvert started out life in politics, became a Member of Parliament (MP) and then a Secretary of State for King James I. An ardent Catholic, he resigned from politics in the mid-1620s and turned his talents towards the colonisation of the New World, where he saw the opportunity to create a refuge for English Catholics.

Interior of St Dunstan-in-the-West

Although he first settled in Avalon off the eastern coast of Canada, he was forced to move due to the somewhat harsh climate to an area further south that later became Maryland. The Royal Charter granted to him was sealed weeks after his death, with his sons carrying on his work. The younger son, Leonard, ultimately became the first colonial governor of the Province of Maryland. Another memorial found here is to **Daniel Brown** of Connecticut, who was the first Anglican clergyman ordained for America in 1723.

In the churchyard there is a bust of **Alfred Harmsworth, Viscount Northcliffe** (1865–1922). A colourful character and great extrovert, Northcliffe was famous for being the pioneer of tabloid journalism; 120 years on, his paper is still publishing the *Daily Mail* in this format. In 1896, its first issue sold almost 400,000 copies more than had ever previously been sold by a newspaper in one day. Northcliffe was indeed a most influential man; in 1917, he headed the British war mission in the United States, for which he was awarded the title Viscount. Although remembered at St Dunstan-in-the-West, he is buried elsewhere in a north London cemetery.

Exit the church and turn left onto Fleet Street. Turn left again at the junction with Fetter Lane. Walk about 40 m (130 ft) along the road.

JOHN WILKES [4]

Here you see a statue of John Wilkes (1727–97), a passionate and outspoken 18th-century journalist, politician and defender of liberty. Born into a middle-class family, he was educated at an academy in Hertford and studied at the University of Leiden in the Dutch Republic.

From a fairly young age, he believed in religious tolerance and was deeply patriotic. He became an MP in 1757 and again in 1761 but was ultimately expelled from Parliament. He later became involved in the politics of the City of London, taking on the role of Alderman, then Sheriff and ultimately Lord Mayor in 1774.

A great champion for democratic rights, Wilkes was opposed to war with the American colonies and spoke publicly against the American Revolutionary War on several occasions. He greatly influenced those campaigning for American independence and the American colonists held him in high

John Wilkes

esteem as a fighter for liberty. Wilkes' brother was the grandfather of US Naval Rear-Admiral and explorer Charles Wilkes.

Thomas Paine (1737–1809), another political activist and revolutionary of the period (and author of *The Rights of Man*), lived on Fetter Lane before becoming involved in the American and French revolutions. It was his writing that is said to have inspired the American rebels to declare independence from Britain.

Cross the road and slightly to your right you will see the entrance to a passageway, Crane Court. Walk through it, stopping in the courtyard.

CRANE COURT [5]

This courtyard was home for much of the 18th century to the most illustrious association of natural philosophers and early scientists, the Royal Society. At that time, members – such as Isaac Newton, Hans Sloane and Joseph Banks – came here to observe scientific demonstrations and hold scholarly debates. The Royal Society's motto – 'Nullius in verba', meaning 'take nobody's word for it' – supported the members' determination to prove statements by looking at the facts and by experiment.

A famous Fellow of the Society was **Benjamin Franklin**, on account of his work with electricity. In fact, he demonstrated the electrical nature of lightning using a key and a kite in a paper to the Royal Society, which is considered by many to be the world's most noted scientific experiment.

In order to advertise a meeting of the Royal Society, a lamp would be hung outside the Fleet Street entrance to the courtyard. Today, if you look above this same entrance, you will see a lamp in the form of an orrery, which is the only reminder of the courtyard's scientific past. Yet, it is still easy to visualise the scene in the Stuart and Georgian City of London when these learned men convened here to discuss their scientific theories.

Crane Court in later years became associated with the publishing industry. It was where the first offices of *Punch* magazine and *The Illustrated London News* were located in the early 1840s.

Turn left down Fleet Street and turn left into the next alleyway, Red Lion Court. This will bring you into Gough Square.

GOUGH SQUARE [6]

The square is the location of the house of 18th-century essayist and wit, Dr Samuel Johnson (1709–84), which today is a museum and open to the public (*Chapter 11).

World famous for producing his comprehensive *Dictionary of the English Language*, Johnson was also fiercely religious (a devout Anglican), an ardent Tory and a great opponent of slavery and of the American Revolution. He wrote

Samuel Johnson's House

Hodge the Cat

pamphlets in defence of government policy and eagerly stated his anti-imperialist views, believing that the English colonists were stealing land from the native American population.

After the death of his wife, Johnson took on a former Caribbean slave, Frank Barber, as his manservant who lived with him for more than 30 years and ultimately became his heir. Johnson opposed slavery on moral grounds and would have applauded the *Abolition of the Slave Trade Act 1807*, which brought about an end to slavery.

_____

Exit Gough Square to the right of the statue of Johnson's cat, Hodge, and follow the alley into Wine Office Court. At the end is the ancient public house:

YE OLDE CHESHIRE CHEESE [7]

Outside the pub in Wine Office Court is a notice explaining the title of the court as well as itemising the many famous literati that have frequented Ye Olde Cheshire Cheese since the 1600s. Writers and poets such as Oliver Goldsmith, Alfred Tennyson, Sir Arthur Conan Doyle, G.K. Chesterton and Dr. Johnson are all said to have been 'regulars'. Despite living very close to the pub in Gough Square, there is no recorded evidence that Dr Johnson ever visited it; however, Charles Dickens was known to be a frequent visitor and readers of *A Tale of Two Cities* will certainly be familiar with the establishment.

In the 19th century, Americans Samuel Langhorne Clemens (aka Mark Twain) and Theodore Roosevelt also took delight in visiting the pub. They enjoyed its association with great literary figures, its dark and somewhat gloomy atmosphere and its range

WINE OFFICE COURT

"SIR" said Dr Johnson "If you wish to have a just notion of the magnitude of this great City you must not be satisfied with seeing its great streets and squares but must survey the innumerable little lanes and courts . . . .

This Court takes it's name from the Excise Office which was here up to 1665. VOLTAIRE came, and, says tradition, CONGREVE and POPE, Dr JOHNSON lived in Gough Square *(End of the Court on the left)* and finished his Great Dictionary there in 1755. OLIVER GOLDSMITH lived at No. 6, where he partly wrote "The Vicar of Wakefield" and Johnson saved him from eviction by selling the book for him . . . .

Here came Johnson's friends: REYNOLDS, GIBBON, GARRICK, Dr BURNEY, BOSWELL and others of his circle.
In the 19th C. came CARLYLE, MACAULAY, TENNYSON DICKENS, *(who mentions the Court in "A Tale of Two Cities")* FORSTER, HOOD, THACKERAY, CRUIKSHANK, LEECH and WILKIE COLLINS. More recently came MARK TWAIN, THEODORE ROOSEVELT, CONAN DOYLE, BEERBOHM CHESTERTON, DOWSON, LE GALEIENE, SYMONS YEATS– and a host of others in search of Dr Johnson, or "The Cheese"

Ye Olde Cheshire Cheese notice

of cosy corners scattered across a number of floors in a maze-like fashion.

Over a century later, Ye Olde Cheshire Cheese is still recognisable from this description and its clientele delight in its many nooks and crannies. It remains a great favourite with visitors and is regarded as being quintessentially British.

Turn left down Fleet Street and stop outside No. 133.

DAILY TELEGRAPH BUILDING [**8**]

This building is currently the London office of the US investment bank Goldman Sachs but it was originally built for the *Daily Telegraph* newspaper in the 1920s. In 1986, the newspaper was purchased by the Hollinger Group and managed by Canadian-born Conrad Black, who moved it out of Fleet Street and into Docklands the following year. He became a British citizen and peer of the realm in 2001, renouncing his Canadian citizenship. Black was later found guilty in the United States of fraud and the obstruction of justice and served time in prison in Florida.

Turn left and at the next junction you will see a black and chrome glass-fronted building at 120 Fleet Street.

DAILY EXPRESS BUILDING [**9**]

Like the previous building, this is now used as offices by Goldman Sachs but was once the home of a major newspaper, the *Daily Express*. Its owner was William Maxwell Aitken (1879–1964), more commonly known as **Lord Beaverbrook**. A Canadian magnate and brilliant publicist, he was involved in the worlds of finance, media and politics. He moved to London in 1910 when he was in his early thirties, having already amassed a small fortune in business in Canada. Within a short time he was elected as an MP in Manchester and shortly afterwards accepted a knighthood. Since childhood, Lord Beaverbrook had had an interest in journalism and slowly but surely – over a period of five or six years – he managed to acquire the *Daily Express* for himself. Under his direction, the paper's circulation increased from 400,000 in 1919 to over 4 million by 1960, thus beating the *Daily Mail* and making the *Daily Express* the highest-selling British newspaper.

Shortly after arriving in London, Lord Beaverbrook developed a strong bond with Prime Minister David Lloyd George, who appreciated his great energy, persuasive powers and talent; he was subsequently made a Minister in the War

Daily Express Building

Cabinet and was one of the very few Ministers to serve again under Winston Churchill during World War II. Lord Beaverbrook took delight in political intrigue and loved to meddle and scheme, playing people off against each another. Yet despite his political manoeuvring and the significant political roles he performed, he is probably acclaimed most for his talent in forming public opinion and his mastery of the newspaper industry.

Now, cross Fleet Street and walk into the small passageway leading to St Bride's Church.

St Bride's Church spire

ST BRIDE'S CHURCH [**10**]

Just before you enter the building, look up at the church spire that was designed by Sir Christopher Wren in 1703, following the Great Fire of London. It is considered one of his most graceful spires, consisting of four octagonal arcades that diminish in size. If it reminds you of a wedding cake with several tiers, you would not be wrong. For, William Rich, a pastry cook living in Fleet Street in the mid-1700s, styled his daughter's wedding cake on the spire. From that time on, this has been the template for countless wedding cakes!

The spire was originally 69 m (226 ft) high and Wren's tallest steeple. Struck by lightning in 1764, it lost 2.4 m (almost 8 ft) – this led to the suggestion that a lightning conductor be installed. The idea was accepted but a debate ensued to decide whether it should it have a blunt or a sharp end. The king, George III, favoured a blunt end. But **Benjamin Franklin**, who had invented the device, wanted a sharp end. The two almost fell out over the matter. In the end, it was the American who won; the blunt, honest King George gave way to the sharp-witted American!

The church owes its name to St Bride, who was born in the 5th century in County Kildare, Ireland. She was renowned for her kindness, hospitality and generosity and was devoted to the Christian faith. There are several churches dedicated to her in the United States, Canada and New Zealand. The present church is the 8th church on the site, which has a history of over 2,000 years. In the crypt there is a Roman pavement, remains of churches from the Saxon and Norman periods and a medieval chapel. Interestingly, these were only found after the destruction of the church in the 1940s, when foundations for the new church were being investigated.

Today's church is very much a working church; services are held daily during the week and twice on Sundays. Lunchtime recitals take place regularly on Tuesdays and Fridays and there are occasional evening concerts too. St Bride's is celebrated worldwide for its excellent music and has a wonderful professional

Plaque to Wynkyn de Worde

choir. Its singers are top musicians with their own international careers and can be heard at Sunday services, weddings, carol services, receptions and memorial services at the church. They produce their own recordings and appear on BBC Radio too.

The church is also known as the 'Journalists' Church'. This is not a recent label but has its roots back in the 16th century. Some 500 years ago, **William Caxton's** assistant, **Wynkyn de Worde**, established his printing press here, marking out St Bride's as the major area for the print industry. He brought his press here because the clergy, being the most literate people in society at the time, were his best customers. More recently, the newspaper industry was based in Fleet Street and so the church has strong and well-established links with the trade. St Bride's is the church where vigils occur for journalists being held hostage overseas. It is also where those working in journalism and the media come to be married or baptised and where funerals and memorial services take place. In 2016, media mogul Rupert Murdoch and American ex-model Jerry Hall (the former wife of Mick Jagger), having married at Spencer House, later celebrated their nuptials at St Bride's with an hour-long church blessing.

The newspaper industry was a major contributor to the restoration of the church after World War II. The beautiful glass doors in the porch, under Wren's archway, were a generous gift from the Press Association.

St Bride's has many American associations. On the south wall is a bust of **Virginia Dare**, who was the first English child to be born in North Carolina, in August 1587. Her parents were married in St Bride's and her grandfather, **John White**, became the Governor of the Roanoke colony. He originally set out for the New World in 1585, landing on Roanoke Island, just off the North Carolina coast, where he drew sketches of the indigenous Indians and flora of the country. After his granddaughter's birth, he returned to England to try to arrange more supplies and settlers for the colony. At

Bust of Virginia Dare

this time England was at war with Spain and, because of the situation, White was unable to return to Roanoke until 1590. When he arrived, the island was totally deserted. Virginia and her family had disappeared and nothing was ever found to explain what had happened to the 'Lost Colony of Roanoke'. The only clue to what had occurred was a word carved on a doorpost, 'Croatoan', the name of a nearby island that was inhabited with friendly natives. The fate of the islanders still remains a mystery. It has never been established whether the settlers died of illness or malnutrition, were perhaps killed by Spanish raiders or grew up among the Indians of North Carolina.

About 30 years later, after a request from the Pilgrim Fathers, St Bride's parish became involved in populating another British colony, Virginia. Some 100 boys and girls who lived in the nearby Bridewell Hospital – orphans with no prospects at home – were sent out to help establish the colony. So successful was this that, three years later, a hundred more orphans joined them. On coming of age, the children all received grants of land. Their descendants, mostly unknowingly, are therefore still linked to this area and to St Bride's.

One of the Pilgrim Fathers, **Edward Winslow**, also had connections with the church. Both he and his parents were married here and he served as a boy apprentice in Fleet Street. He sailed with his wife on the *Mayflower* in 1620 and later became (three times) Governor of Plymouth, Massachusetts. It is to his and the endeavours of the other Pilgrim Fathers that the 1957 English oak reredos behind the altar is dedicated. It is truly a very fine freestanding screen, carved in the style of Grinling Gibbons and decorated with eight flambeaux.

The Journalist's Altar on the north-east side of the church is dedicated to journalists and media workers in trouble spots around the world. On display are tributes to the dedication and bravery of these men and women as well as memorials to reporters and cameramen who have been killed carrying out their work abroad. There is a plaque on the north wall commemorating the vigils that were kept here during the 1980s, when John McCarthy and Terry Anderson were kept in Lebanon as hostages. After 9/11, a memorial service was held here for journalists and again on the first anniversary of the event. Indeed, the church has become a centre for journalists from every religion and continent.

On one of the stalls near the Journalist's Altar, there is a plaque that remembers US journalists who have given their lives in duty overseas (presented by the Overseas Press Club of America). Another plaque bears a memorial to the **Reverend Holt Souter** of Richmond, Virginia, who was the Guild Chaplain at St Bride's between 1986 and 1995.

Return to Fleet Street and turn right. At the road junction, cross over Farringdon Street and walk up Ludgate Hill on the left-hand side of the street towards St Paul's Cathedral. Take the second turning on the left into Old Bailey. Walk until you see the court entrance on the right-hand side of the road.

THE OLD BAILEY [11]

Formally titled the Central Criminal Court, the Old Bailey is a definite icon of the area and has been the major criminal court in London for hundreds of years. Until the early 20th century it was home to Newgate Prison, which throughout its history had been notorious for brutality, the harshness of its conditions, its overcrowding and the spread of disease.

Although never incarcerated, **William Penn** (who went on to found Pennsylvania) was brought to trial here in the 1670s, along with fellow Quaker **William Mead**. Their offence was that they addressed an unlicensed assembly (contravening an Act of Parliament declaring the prohibition of public worship outside the Church of England). The jury refused to convict the two men and this led to the jurors being incarcerated in jail for two days. On their release, the jurors were fined for returning a 'not guilty' verdict, which resulted in the establishment of the right of juries to give a verdict according to their consciences. The case thus became a legal landmark and is commemorated today on a plaque within the Old Bailey courthouse.

Many famous trials have taken place here over the centuries, including that of authors Daniel Defoe, Oscar Wilde and Jeffrey Archer; East end villains the Kray twins; Yorkshire Ripper Peter Sutcliffe; and Soham murderer Ian Huntley.

The building is mentioned in the children's nursery rhyme 'Oranges and Lemons', as well as in many novels ranging from Charles Dickens' *A Tale of Two Cities* to Jeffrey Archer's *A Prisoner of Birth*. It is also frequently depicted in films and on television (*Chapter 6).

Continue along the street to the junction. Cross over Newgate Street and turn left into Holburn Viaduct, passing beside the churchyard. The church entrance is beneath its tower.

St Sepulchre Without
Newgate Church

ST SEPULCHRE-WITHOUT-NEWGATE [12]

Commonly known as St Sepulchre's, the church takes its name from the Church of the Holy Sepulchre in Jerusalem. It was built just outside the north-west gate of the Roman city of London. It is from here that the knights of the Crusades began their journey to the Holy Land.

Nowadays, St Sepulchre's is the largest parish church in the Square Mile and has a tower, porch and walls dating back to the mid-15th century. (Its pinnacles, however, were added in Victorian times.) Gutted by fire in 1666, the church was immediately rebuilt by Joshua Marshall, one of Sir Christopher Wren's master masons, but has undergone much restoration over the centuries, resulting in somewhat of an architectural hotchpotch inside.

Naturally, being a stone's throw away from Newgate Prison, there has been a long association between the church and the jail. It is said that underground tunnels once existed between the two, through which the clergy would visit the condemned prisoners before their execution at the gallows. From 1605, it was customary to ring a bell outside the prisoners' cells at midnight the night before an execution and then the bellringer would shout out the following advice:

All you that in the condemned hole do lie,
Prepare you, for tomorrow you shall die.
Watch all, and pray: the hour is drawing near,
That you before the Almighty must appear.
Examine well yourselves, in time repent,
That you may not to eternal flames be sent,
And when St. Sepulchre's Bell in the morning tolls,
The Lord above have mercy on your souls.
        PAST TWELVE O'CLOCK'

The execution hand bell can be seen in a glass case to the south of the nave.

Window in the Musician's Chapel

As with many of the City churches, St Sepulchre's is known for its musical excellence and has been the official musicians' church for many years. It boasts a fine-looking 1670 Renatus Harris organ in the north aisle that George Frideric Handel, Felix Mendelssohn and Samuel Wesley all played, although sadly it is no longer in use today. Beside the organ is the Musician's Chapel, which is where **Sir Henry Wood**, the founder of the annual BBC Promenade Concerts, is buried. Wood learned to play the organ in the church and was appointed Assistant Organist at just 14 years of age! His ashes lie beneath the central window, which depicts him both as a young boy at the organ and as the mature Sir Henry conducting a Promenade Concert at the Queen's Hall. Australian soprano Dame Nellie Melba also has a window dedicated to her in the chapel.

St Sepulchre's is particularly associated with **Captain John Smith** (1580–1631), who was to become the first Governor of Virginia. Smith was born in the area, worshipped at the church and took Communion here. He died in a house close by and his remains are in the south aisle of the church, although the exact position of the tomb is unknown as it was destroyed during the Great Fire in 1666.

Born in the middle of Queen Elizabeth I's reign, a time of swashbuckling and exploration, Smith was a very colourful character. He is best known today for his association with **Pocahontas**, who rescued him from death. An inveterate adventurer, he had many exploits in his youth as a mercenary soldier in Asia, Europe and Africa. Legend says that after decapitating three Turkish officers single-handedly, he was granted a coat of arms with 'Three Turks' heads couped'.

On the south wall, you can see a beautiful modern stained-glass window dedicated to Smith, a gift of his biographer, Bradford Smith. Captain Smith's heraldic device, the trio of heads, is at the top, while at the bottom are the *Discovery*, *Godspeed* and *Susan Constant*, the three ships that sailed for Virginia from London in December 1606. Captain Smith is the figure in the central panel, shown with navigational instruments around his feet. The outer panels depict his two patrons and above all three are their coats of arms.

John Smith's greatest claims to fame were his adventures in Virginia in 1607. His resourcefulness and energy singled him out as leader of Jamestown. He explored territory in and around Chesapeake Bay, traded with the Indians for food, enforced order and established work for the settlers. Subsequently, he was honoured by becoming President of the Council of Virginia and Admiral of New England.

St Sepulchre's has one other important American connection: it was here that the christening took place of the founder of Rhode Island, **Roger Williams** (c.1603–83). As the parish records were destroyed during the Great Fire in 1666, his exact date of birth is unconfirmed but it is known that he was educated at Charterhouse School and Pembroke College, Cambridge, and later ordained as a deacon in the Church of England. On discovering Puritanism (not tolerated under King Charles I), he decided to start

Window depicting Captain John Smith

a new life and set sail for the American colonies, arriving with his wife in Boston in 1631. In time, he fell out with the local community on account of his views on religious toleration. He purchased land from the native Indians and founded a new colony, Rhode Island, based upon principles of religious liberty, political democracy and the separation of church and state, all principles that would later be adopted in the US constitution.

Exit the church and turn left into Giltspur Street. Walk along and turn right into West Smithfield. Pass by the entrance to St Bartholomew's Hospital. You will see a Tudor-style half-timbered gateway directly ahead. This is the entrance to St Bartholomew the Great church.

ST BARTHOLOMEW THE GREAT [13]

The buildings of the former priory were partly dismantled in 1539 during the turbulent period of the Dissolution of the Monasteries. Later, when Queen Elizabeth I came to the throne, St Bartholomew's became a parish church, although reduced in size. In the following years, the north transept was used as a blacksmith's forge; a school and stable were established and the Lady Chapel was transformed into a printing works in the 18th century. It was here in the early 1720s that **Benjamin Franklin**, later venerated as one of America's Founding Fathers, worked for a brief period as a journeyman printer. He was an early and relentless campaigner for colonial unity and not only wrote against the authority of British rule in the colonies but also acted as a spokesman for several of them whilst in London. Besides being a political theorist, he was also an active diplomat and statesman, becoming America's first Ambassador to France after the American Revolution. Franklin spent a good deal of time in London in the mid-1700s and throughout the period was much admired as a leading author, politician, scientist and inventor.

St Bartholomew the Great is one of the City of London's most famous churches largely because of its wonderfully preserved Norman round arches, its piers and heavy columns. Such an example of Norman architecture (apart from St John's chapel in the Tower of London) is almost unique in London.

Within the church on the south side is the 15th-century font, where famous painter, printmaker and social critic William Hogarth was baptised in 1697. Church founder Rahere's magnificent highly coloured tomb is located close to the altar on the north side of the sanctuary.

Lady Chapel at St Bartholomew the Great

This completes the tour at the western edge of the Square Mile. Farringdon underground station (Hammersmith & City, Circle and Metropolitan lines) is a short stroll away.

If you still have time and stamina, then make your way over to the Tower Hill area *(you can take the tube from Farringdon to Tower Hill)*, where you will discover further interesting associations between the City of London and the United States.

Begin your walk just outside Tower Hill underground station (Circle, District lines), within Trinity Square Gardens.

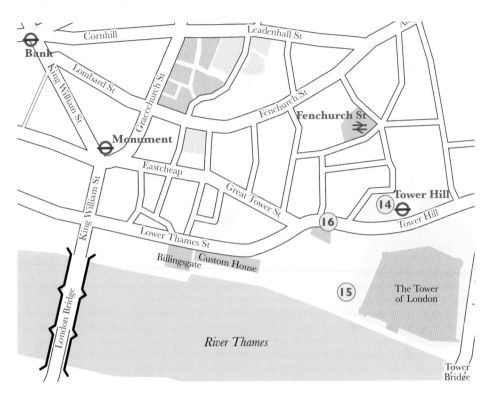

TRINITY SQUARE GARDENS [14]

It was at a site here (around 43 Trinity Square) that **William Penn** (1644–1718) was born. His father, Admiral Sir William Penn, had been knighted by King Charles II as a reward for taking part in the king's restoration in 1660 and the Penn family was held in high regard. Admiral Penn was a powerful and influential man, a landowner, politician and Commissioner of the Navy, while his wife was the daughter of a rich merchant from Rotterdam. In the 1660s, while Admiral Penn was working at the Navy Office in Seething Lane, the Penn family lived next door to **Samuel Pepys**

(1633–1703) and his wife. Pepys at this time was the chief administrator of the Navy Board (Clerk of the Acts to the Kings' Ships) and worked hard to bring about a much more efficient and less corrupt Navy. Pepys got to know Admiral Penn well and refers to him on several occasions in his famous book *The Diary of Samuel Pepys*.

Now, walk through the gardens and cross the road over to the Tower of London. Stop either in the main piazza (by the ticket booths) or on the quayside beside the Thames.

TOWER OF LONDON [15]

Sir Walter Raleigh (c.1552–1618), the noted Elizabethan explorer, soldier, politician and courtier, sailed to America in 1578 with his half-brother and explorer Sir Humphrey Gilbert. This expedition is said to have inspired him to invest in an English colony there in the 1580s. The colony he established was near Roanoke Island (on the coast of present-day North Carolina) and became known as 'Virginia' in honour of his patron, Elizabeth I (known as the Virgin Queen). Although Raleigh never actually set foot in North America he led an expedition to South America in the 1590s and again in 1616, searching for 'El Dorado', the mythical land of gold, but neither trip resulted in success.

Raleigh was said to be the most entertaining, dashing and charismatic character. He was a great favourite of Elizabeth I, who granted him a knighthood in 1587. She also showered him with trade privileges and an Irish estate and appointed him Captain of the Queen's Guard.

Nonetheless the queen, in a fit of jealousy, had Raleigh and his new wife incarcerated in the Tower of London when she discovered that he had secretly married one of her ladies-in-waiting. Although only briefly imprisoned in the Tower, it took time for Raleigh to ingratiate himself again with the queen and to regain her trust and favour. After Elizabeth I's death in 1603, Raleigh was confined once again in the Tower, having been found guilty of treason and condemned to death by King James I. He spent 13 years living inside the fortress's forbidding walls before his sentence was eventually carried out in 1618.

If you would like to see the reconstructed Raleigh rooms in the Bloody Tower, buy a ticket to the attraction online (www.hrp.org.uk) or from the ticket office at the piazza. The Tower of London is a UNESCO World Heritage Site and opens daily between 10 a.m and 6 p.m.

Exit the piazza by Tower Hill and turn immediately left. Enter the church through the glass doorway.

ALL HALLOWS BY THE TOWER [16]

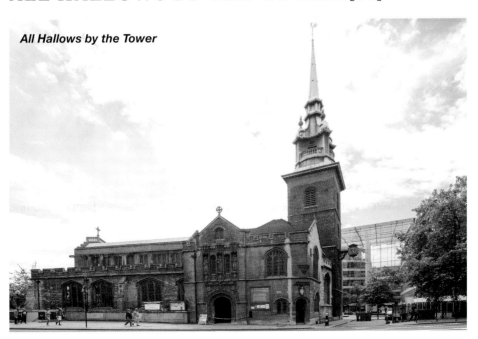

All Hallows by the Tower

This church is the oldest in the Square Mile and worship has taken place here for more than 1,300 years. In 1666, during the Great Fire of London, All Hallows was saved from certain devastation by the quick-thinking actions of Admiral Penn and Samuel Pepys, who organised the demolition of many nearby houses to provide a firebreak. The Admiral's son, **William**, was baptised here on 23 October 1644 and educated in the schoolroom. The actual record of his birth is displayed on the old church register in the museum crypt.

In 1681, King Charles II granted William a land charter, which he named 'Pennsylvania', to repay an outstanding debt of £16,000 to William's father. William became the governor and proprietor of the new colony and moved there in 1682, writing its constitution, establishing good relations with the local Indian tribes and allocating land to settlers. Run as a Quaker colony, Pennsylvania

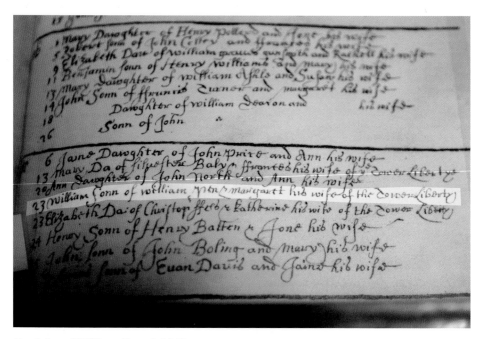

Register of William Penn's birth

became attractive to Quakers from all over Europe as well as people seeking religious tolerance. Although he lived in the colony at various times throughout his life, William spent his final years back in England, leaving the colony governed by deputy governors along with his secretary.

Another display of interest in the crypt is the Marriage Register entry dated 26 July 1797 of the sixth President of the United States, **John Quincy Adams** (1767–1848) and Louisa Catherine Johnson. Until recent times, Louisa was the only American First Lady to have been born outside the United States. She no longer holds this position, as President Donald Trump's wife, Melania, was born in Slovenia.

All Hallows still retains strong links with the United States today, especially with the Church of the Epiphany in New York and Christ Church in Philadelphia. The church is open seven days a week and serves both the local City community and the many visitors to the Tower Hill area.

The tour ends here and you will find many cafes, restaurants and pubs nearby. The closest underground station is Tower Hill (Circle, District lines).

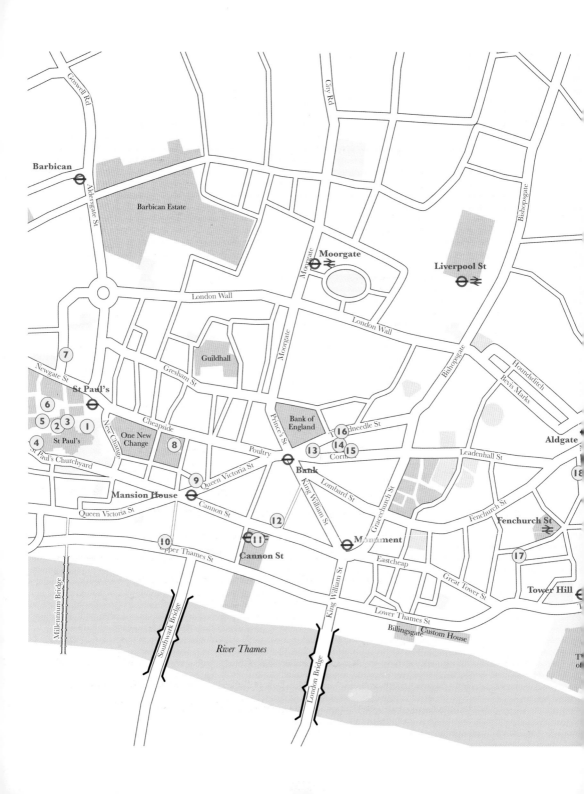

PERSONALITIES, PHILANTHROPISTS, MONUMENTS AND MEMORIALS

This walk introduces you to some of the people associated with the Square Mile by means of public sculptures, monuments and artworks.

Start at St Paul's underground station (Central line) and cross over into the cathedral churchyard. You will see a tall column immediately in front of you.

ST PAUL'S CROSS [1]

St Paul's Cross

The large column dates from the early 1900s and replaces a much earlier cross that had stood on a spot nearby for close to eight centuries until it was destroyed in 1643. The cross was sometimes referred to as St Paul's Preaching Cross due to the many sermons given at this spot by the clergy. It was also where the population assembled to hear what was happening in London and in the country and where announcements were made about victories in battles at sea and on land.

St Paul's Cross was the place where citizens learned about royal births, marriages and deaths, where papal bulls and edicts were handed down, national addresses given and where religious and secular announcements were delivered. It was, in effect, the news and social media of its day. By the late 1400s, it had become one of the City's most ornate structures. A spacious timber pulpit with a lead roof, reached by a flight of stone steps. Eventually destroyed during the Puritan rule of the mid-17th century, it was never rebuilt. A floor plaque along the pathway beside the east end of the cathedral is the only reminder today of the original St Paul's Cross.

Walk through the churchyard with the cathedral on your left. In about 30 m (100 ft) you will see a monument on the right.

JOHN WESLEY'S STATUE [2]

This statue of John Wesley (1703–91) is said to bear a remarkable likeness to the man, who was renowned for his relentless preaching and the establishment of the worldwide Methodist church. It depicts him as a dapper, disciplined gentleman in the austere dress of his day and is a copy of a statue made for but never erected in Westminster Abbey, as the clergy of the time did not approve of his religious doctrines.

Born into a poor Lincolnshire family, Wesley's father was a rector and both parents were devoutly Protestant. It's not surprising then that he should form a group of theologians while studying at Oxford, which became known as the 'Methodists' for adhering to a methodical religious existence.

After a brief yet unsuccessful visit as a missionary to America, Wesley returned to the City of London and had a profound religious experience in May 1738. Subsequently, he preached sermons all around the country, many to outdoor gatherings, and soon he had a substantial following. He worked with his brother Charles to bring and share their beliefs with others; John organised the movement, while Charles wrote many hymns. Thus the Methodist Church was born. John's sermons formed the doctrinal basis for the Church that grew in popularity daily.

Thousands were converted to Christianity because of him, many of whom came from the working class previously excluded from the Church on account of their class.

In the latter part of his life, John Wesley lived in City Road on the City of London's northernmost boundary, a short walk from this spot. He is remembered today both within this churchyard and in his City Road Chapel and home (both open to the public), as well as on a plaque that commemorates his conversion, situated beside the entrance to the Museum of London.

John Wesley

Turn around to view:

PEOPLE OF LONDON MEMORIAL [3]

Cut from a single block of limestone, this round memorial was unveiled by the late Her Majesty Queen Elizabeth The Queen Mother in 1999. It is the result of a campaign by the *Evening Standard* newspaper to remember the 30,000 Londoners who lost their lives during the World War II bombing raids. Subscriptions received from the public paid for its erection and the memorial was designed by Richard Kindersley (of the Dorling Kindersley publishing family). The words inscribed on its surface – 'In War Resolution; In Defeat Defiance; In Victory Magnanimity; In Peace

Goodwill' – were cited by Winston Churchill in the frontispiece of his history of World War II, although they were written by Sir Edward Marsh after World War I.

Exit the churchyard and walk towards the front of the cathedral. Stop opposite the main entrance.

QUEEN ANNE STATUE [4]

When St Paul's was completed in 1711, Queen Anne (1665–1714) was the reigning monarch and this accounts for her marble statue outside the cathedral. The monument shows Queen Anne standing with her back to the church and surrounded by four female statues representing America, Ireland, France and England, countries under her domain at the time. Look closely at the Royal Coat of Arms and see that it contains the French fleur-de-lis, the English lion and the Irish harp. As to why the Queen faces away from the church, this is best explained in a ditty left on the statue by a wit, referring to her fondness for drink:

Brandy Nan, Brandy Nan,
left in the lurch
Her face to the gin-shop,
her back to the church.

Queen Anne statue

Anne was the last Stuart monarch and sadly died without an heir, although not for want of trying. She had 17 pregnancies but not one child survived. Under the terms of the *Act of Settlement 1701*, her second cousin, George I of the House of Hanover, succeeded her to the throne.

Turn left and walk towards:

TEMPLE BAR GATE [5]

The gateway you can see is Sir Christopher Wren's Portland stone gate, **Temple Bar Gate**, a structure that marked the entrance to the City of London for 200 years. Originally it straddled the Strand but towards the end of the 19th century the archway became too narrow for the traffic and the monument was taken down stone by stone in 1877. It was then rebuilt at Theobold's Park in Hertfordshire, to form a grand entrance to a country estate. In 2001, the City of London agreed to help fund the restoration of the historic gate and to bring it back to the City, placing it as the main entrance to the newly reconstructed Paternoster Square.

Before its return from Hertfordshire, Temple Bar Gate's stonework and four royal statues

Temple Bar Gate

(of Charles I, Charles II, James I and Anne of Denmark) were renovated, while new statues of royal beasts, city supporters and associated coats of arms were added to the monument to bring it back to its former glory. Today, in addition to providing the main entrance to Paternoster Square from St Paul's Cathedral, Temple Bar Gate also hires out its upstairs rooms as venues for receptions and business meetings.

Pass through the gate into:

PATERNOSTER SQUARE [6]

The square is built on the site that, from the Middle Ages, had been the very heart of the publishing, book and stationery industries. Due to severe damage during wartime bombing, it was rebuilt in the immediate aftermath of World War II. At the time, money was in short supply, the range of building materials were limited and emphasis was not generally placed on design. The postwar modernist square was never popular; proposals were put forward for its redevelopment but nothing changed until the mid-1990s, when a new masterplan for the site was proposed and the 1960s square was subsequently demolished. Designers of the new development took great care to fit it in with its surroundings, especially with its neighbour, St Paul's Cathedral and also reintroduced the ancient street pattern around Paternoster Square. Architectural firm Whitfield Partners also chose to enhance the public space by adding several new pieces of art.

The most obvious of these is the monument that you see immediately as you enter the square: an imposing 23 m (75 ft) high Corinthian column. Made of Portland stone, it has a striking gold leaf-covered flaming urn at its top and is a copy of a 17th-century design by the architect Inigo Jones for the front of the cathedral. The designers have cleverly used the column to mask a ventilation shaft for a car park and road built beneath the square and added a water feature too.

Behind the column and above the main entrance to the London Stock Exchange, you can see a modern sundial, *Noon Mark*. The work of The Cardozo Kindersley Workshop, it casts its shadow to show which day of the year it is when seen in bright sunlight at midday. *Noon Mark* is said to represent the working of the three main global Stock Markets: as the Stock Exchange closes in London, another one opens in New York, and when that shuts down, the one in Tokyo takes over.

To the left of the square is a stainless-steel artwork by Thomas Heatherwick (famous for his design of the modern Routemaster bus) called *Angel's Wings*. At 11 m (36 ft) in height, the structure skilfully disguises two air vents above an electricity substation.

Cross the square and you will find Elisabeth Frink's bronze sculpture entitled *Shepherd and Sheep.* Originally commissioned for the postwar Paternoster Square development, it was unveiled by master violinist and conductor Yehudi Menuhin in 1975.

From here, walk through the shopping area ahead. Take the first alleyway on your left and proceed to Newgate Street. Cross the road into King Edward Street, passing by Christchurch Greyfriars Church Garden on the left. Stop by the statue to Rowland Hill.

ROWLAND HILL [7]

This statue stands in front of the former General Post Office building and remembers the man who was responsible for introducing the 'Penny Post' – Rowland Hill (1795–1879). The idea for a one-penny prepaid postal system came to him in the 1830s at a time when recipients paid the postage costs, which varied according to the distance and how much paper was included! Implemented in 1840 and the only one in the world at that time, his postal system is still in use throughout the United Kingdom today – although the stamps are now self-adhesive.

Apart from reforming the postal system, Hill was also an able administrator and an educationalist. Influenced by his father's close friend, liberal scientist Joseph Priestley, Hill became a teacher and set up his own school using Priestley's methods. Subsequently, he worked as Secretary in the South Australian Colonisation Commission and wrote the paper setting out his ideas for postal reforms while there. His system was a great success in his own lifetime and earned him a knighthood as well as a burial spot within Westminster Abbey.

Rowland Hill

Cross over King Edward Street into Angel Street directly ahead. Turn right at the junction with St-Martin's-le-Grand and walk to the end of the road. Turn left into Cheapside. In about 100 m (330 ft) you will see a church on the right. Cross Cheapside into St Mary-le-Bow churchyard.

JOHN SMITH [8]

This bronze memorial is to Captain John Smith (1580–1631), who in 1608 became the first Governor of Virginia. Born in the area around Cheapside, Smith was a most colourful character, a soldier, a mercenary and an adventurer.

At 26 years of age, he set sail for America with three ships in order to set up a colony there. It was a very difficult voyage and Smith argued so badly with the captain and crew that they imprisoned him and intended to kill him. Fortunately, his employers, the Virginia Company, saved him from this fate and appointed Smith as one of the members of the colony's council. Smith went on to establish Jamestown but was unfortunate then to be captured by one of the native tribes. It is believed that it was only due to the intervention of the chief's young daughter, Pocahontas, that his life was spared (it is said that she put her head on Smith's, preventing her father from executing him).

In 1609, Smith returned to England, singing the colony's praises, and he became its greatest supporter. After a further two voyages to New England, he settled back in London where he wrote accounts of the great daring adventures he had experienced on his travels. Contrary to popular belief, Captain Smith and Pocahontas never married, although she did wed another Englishman, tobacco planter John Rolfe. They travelled to London in 1616 but very sadly she died in Gravesend the following year, having become quite a celebrity during her brief stay in the country.

Captain John Smith memorial

Captain Smith's statue was placed in the St Mary-le-Bow churchyard as it falls within the Ward of Cordwainer (one of the City of London's 25 wards) and the cavalier captain was a member of the Cordwainer Company. Cordwainer is not a name in common usage today; it derives from Córdoba (also known as Cordova) in Spain, where the finest medieval leather was produced. Cordwainers make new shoes from new leather, which is quite different to a cobbler, who repairs shoes. To emphasise the Cordovan connection, the granite paving laid down in the yard has a pattern that reflects Cordovan influences from the Mezquita in Córdoba.

Walk to the far end of the churchyard piazza and turn left beside the church. This will bring you into Bow Lane, where you turn right. At the junction ahead, turn left into Watling Street. Stop beside the wall of St Mary Aldermary church.

CORDWAINER STATUE [**9**]

Here you see a wonderful depiction of a seated Cordwainer. Sculptor Alma Boyes produced the bronze piece in 2002 to mark the 100th anniversary of the Cordwainer Ward Club. Geographically, the ward is one of the smallest in the City of London, being a mere 270 m (886 ft) long and 130 m (427 ft) wide, wedged between Cheapside and Cannon Street.

Today, the Cordwainers, like many other livery companies, support their industry through the provision of scholarships, grants and bursaries. In this way, they continue to promote the shoe industry in the United Kingdom. The Cordwainers have fostered a strong relationship with the London College of Fashion, where many shoe designers have been trained. Jimmy Choo and L.K. Bennett are both members of the Company.

Cordwainer statue

Continue down Bow Lane to the major junction with Queen Victoria Street and Cannon Street. Cross the junction into Garlick Hill (directly in front of you) and walk to the end of the street. In front of you is an unusual statue:

SWAN MARKER AND BARGE MASTER [**10**]

Believed to be the first public sculpture in London ever to be commissioned by a livery company, this excellent 2007 artwork by Vivien Mallock is installed beside St James Garlickhythe church. The Vintners' Company, which commissioned the

piece, shares the annual duty of 'swan marking' on the River Thames with the Dyers' Company. Here you see the Vintners' Barge Master in his traditional costume, with a swan at his feet.

Retrace your steps back to Cannon Street and turn right. Walk along until you reach Cannon Street station and climb the stairs towards the platform. The memorial is beside Platform 4, next to the station's Arrival and Departure indicator board.

Swan Marker and Barge Master

PLUMBER'S APPRENTICE MEMORIAL [11]

Placed at the railway terminus in 2011, Martin Jennings' sculpture was commissioned to mark the completion of Cannon Street station's renovation as well as the 400th anniversary of the granting of the Plumbers' Royal Charter. The 2.1 m (7 ft) tall bronze statue represents the industry's history within the City of London and The Worshipful Company of Plumbers' commitment to training young plumbers.

Chris Sneath, Master of The Worshipful Company of Plumbers, said, 'The statue is as much about promoting plumbing as a worthy career for young people as it is about marking our ancient connections with the City of London.' The Plumbers' Hall had existed on the site beside the station until it was compulsorily purchased in 1863 to allow for the expansion of the station.

Retrace your steps into Cannon Street and cross over the road. Turn right and stop just before St Swithin's Lane, outside 111 Cannon Street.

LONDON STONE [12]

At the time of writing, this ancient London landmark is lodged at the Museum of London while a new office development is being constructed on the site but it is due to be returned to its home here early in 2018. London Stone, whose provenance is unknown, is usually set in the wall of 111 Cannon Street. Some say it dates back to the Roman era and was once a stone used to measure road distances, others believe that it comes from Saxon London. Certainly, for hundreds of years it was of such great importance that deals were struck, formal declarations made and legislation enacted before it.

The stone was first referenced in the 1100s. Its original purpose has never been established but many believe it to be of great historical significance or to have mystical powers. What is known is that it was once a much larger object and that it has been moved backwards and forwards across Cannon Street on a number of occasions.

Walk along Cannon Street with the station on your left and turn right into Walbrook. When you reach Bank junction, cross over to the island. The monument to the Duke of Wellington sits in front of the Royal Exchange, facing No.1 Poultry.

DUKE OF WELLINGTON STATUE [13]

Arthur Wellesley, 1st Duke of Wellington (1769–1852) is undoubtedly one of the nation's most celebrated military heroes. He made his mark leading overseas campaigns at the end of the 18th century and the beginning of the 19th century. These campaigns culminated in his defeat of Napoleon at the Battle of Waterloo in 1815.

The Duke's equestrian statue was placed outside the Royal Exchange after its reopening in 1844 and unveiled on the anniversary of the Battle of Waterloo. Cast in bronze (extracted from captured enemy cannons during his military campaigns), the sculpture is attributed mainly to Sir Francis Chantrey and received a mixed reception largely on account of the lack of stirrups and saddle as well as the Duke's attire (out of military uniform and without a hat!). When the Duke died in 1852, crowds filled the City's streets to pay their last respects and St Paul's Cathedral was filled to the brim with mourners attending his funeral service.

Walk along Cornhill to the right of the main entrance to the Royal Exchange, past the row of shops, and stop at the far end of the building.

SIR THOMAS GRESHAM [14]

The brainchild of Sir Thomas Gresham, the Royal Exchange was built during the reign of Queen Elizabeth I and modelled on the Bourse in Antwerp. A wealthy merchant and royal financial adviser, Gresham had been impressed by the Belgian Bourse, which allowed merchants to meet within a building and conduct their day-to-day business unimpeded by the vagaries of the weather outside. The Exchange was built in 1566 as London's first specialist commercial building for trading stocks and officially opened by Queen Elizabeth I in 1571, when she conferred the title 'Royal' upon it. The present building, designed by Sir William Tite, is the third on the site and dates from the mid-19th century. (*Chapter 2).

Thomas Gresham's grasshopper sign

High up on the clock tower on the building's easternmost side is William Behnes' statue of Gresham, and if you glance up above the tower, you will see a striking golden weathervane in the shape of Gresham's family emblem, a grasshopper. As Gresham was highly influential within the Square Mile, his name crops up often across the City: for instance, in nearby Gresham Street and at the site of Gresham Bank (illustrated by the Gresham grasshopper sign) in Lombard Street.

In his lifetime, Sir Thomas Gresham was held in great esteem by the Tudor monarchs and acted as agent for King Henry VIII, King Edward VI and Edward's half-sister, Queen Elizabeth I. When he died without an heir, much of his accumulated wealth was bequeathed to the City and led to the creation in 1597 of London's first higher-education institution, Gresham College. The college is still going strong today and offers free education from its 14th-century base in Barnard's Inn Hall, Holborn.

Now look at the stone memorial at ground level.

PAUL JULIUS REUTER MEMORIAL [15]

When Paul Julius Reuter arrived in London in the mid-19th century, he very quickly revolutionised the way in which financial news could be delivered to world traders in the City of London. He brought with him a well-tried-out system from Belgium, where he'd used a mixture of a fleet of carrier pigeons and new telegraph cables to deliver stock prices and news. This service was acknowledged immediately for its reliability and, moreover, for its fast delivery and objectivity.

Reuter's first office was based close by at 1 Royal Exchange Buildings, the reason for his monument here behind the Royal Exchange. Reuter later moved into Fleet Street alongside and amid the multitude of newspaper offices and printworks. As new technology impacted upon the industry, the company ultimately followed

Paul Julius Reuter memorial

its fellow newspaper companies and moved eastwards into the newly built offices in Docklands.

By employing the fastest and newest technology, Reuter was able to provide news in advance of his competitors. In 1865, the news of President Abraham Lincoln's assassination reached London via a Reuter's report much earlier than in Continental Europe and consequently caused chaos in many of their financial markets.

In the 21st century Reuters remains one of the world's major financial information and service companies. It supplies the most up-to-the-minute information on all types of financial records, bonds, equities and derivatives as well as historical information on thousands of companies. Governments, the media and individual businesses all rely upon the organisation (which has been part of Thomson Reuters financial and risk division since 2008), not only for its financial news but also for its information and news provision and services.

Turn right towards Threadneedle Street to see:

GEORGE PEABODY STATUE [**16**]

George Peabody, a merchant banker and great philanthropist, was born in Danvers, Massachusetts, and lived in London from 1837. In 1862, he gave huge monies to London's poor and set up a trust to provide dwellings for the honest and decent 'working classes' but not for the destitute. His estates, many of which still exist today, were all built in very distinctive yellow London brick and were dry, clean and healthy allowing workers the chance to live close to their workplace and to pay a reasonable rent. Those earning too high a salary did not qualify for housing, while those in casual work would not be offered housing as their income was not sufficiently stable. Strict rules stated that residents had to be vaccinated against smallpox and take their turn in cleaning the communal

George Peabody statue

passages and lavatories. Although far from perfect, it was a good step forward and many other philanthropists followed his lead (Guinness, Sutton Housing Trust).

A legend in his own lifetime, Peabody was buried in Westminster Abbey after a funeral attended by Queen Victoria and the Prince of Wales. Only three weeks later, however, his body was exhumed and returned to the United States for burial in his hometown of Danvers, the southern section of which was renamed Peabody in his honour.

Walk back to Cornhill and turn left. Walk straight ahead, crossing over Gracechurch Street and into Leadenhall Street. Walk past the Lloyd's Building and The Scalpel and then turn right down Billiter Street. Walk the length of the street and cross over Fenchurch Street into Mark Lane directly ahead. Take the 2nd turning on the left into Hart Street.

ST OLAVE HART STREET [17]

Famous 17th-century diarist **Samuel Pepys** lived in Seething Lane, close to St Olave, while he worked nearby at the Navy Office as Clerk of the Acts to the Kings' Ships. He and his wife, Elizabeth, were important parishioners in the congregation and both have memorials within the church, although they are not beside each another. Elizabeth's bust within an oval niche is located above the north side of the altar, while her husband is remembered on a portrait roundel in the south aisle. There is no indication of their place of burial beneath the High Altar.

St Olave Hart Street churchyard entrance

It is said that the church escaped the ravages of the Great Fire of London in 1666 due to the prompt action by Pepys and Admiral Sir William Penn (father of William Penn, who founded Pennsylvania) in demolishing nearby buildings to establish a firebreak. Three centuries later, St Olave suffered great damage during World War II but was very well restored to its original style in the 1950s and remains a truly excellent example of a medieval City parish church. Its gateway is easy to recognise, as it has ghostly skulls (these led Charles Dickens to rename the church St Ghastly Grim in *The Uncommercial Traveller*).

The church is dedicated to King Olaf of Norway, who fought against the Danish invaders in the early 11th century alongside the English monarch, Ethelred the Unready. It was because of Olaf's actions that the Danes failed to cross the Thames and the event became the basis of the nursery rhyme 'London Bridge is Falling Down'.

Continue along Hart Street and cross Seething Lane into Crutched Friars. Follow the road for about 5 minutes, after which it changes name to Jewry Street. You will see the Cass Foundation on your right, just before you reach Aldgate High Street.

SIR JOHN CASS STATUE [18]

Sir John Cass (1661–1718) was a wealthy merchant born in the Portsoken Ward of the City. In his lifetime, he held several political posts (as Member of Parliament for the City, and also as Sheriff and Alderman). In addition, he was appointed the Master of the Skinners' and Carpenters' Companies at various times.

Extremely passionate about education, John Cass supported both a local parochial school and established a school for poor children. Some 30 years after his death, the Cass Foundation was set up and it still functions today as an independent charity supporting a range of educational establishments, from

Sir John Cass statue

preschool to university level, seven of which bear the Cass name.

The building on Jewry Street is headquarters to the Cass Foundation, which is celebrated for its grants to schools and educational bodies as well as to individual and students. It continues Cass' vision and his philanthropy by providing support to projects that benefit young people from disadvantaged backgrounds living in inner London. Look up high on the front of the building to see, sitting within a niche, a striking statue of John Cass dressed in his Alderman's robes. This is a replica of the original by Louis-François Roubiliac (which is now at Guildhall).

This is the end of the walk. Turn right at Aldgate High Street and cross over the road. You will find Aldgate underground station (Circle, Metropolitan lines) about 20 m (65 ft) further along the street.

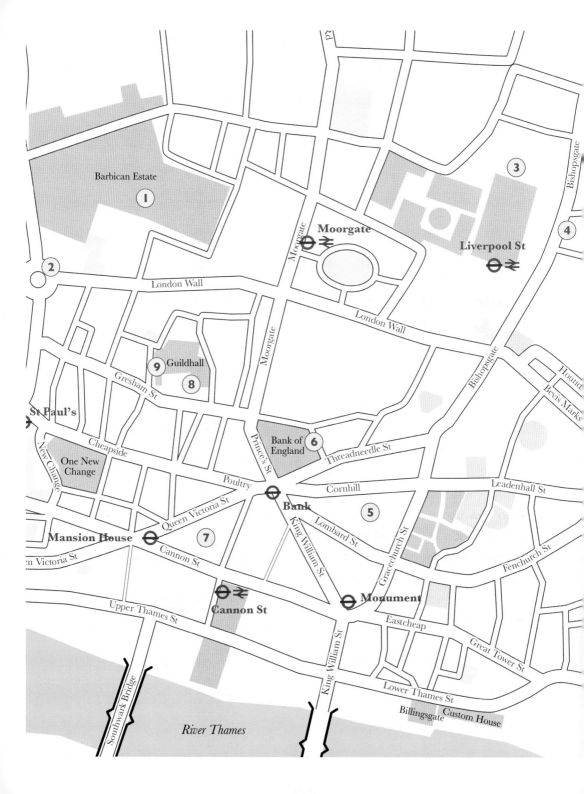

Barbican Estate

(1)

(3)

(4)

(2)

Moorgate

Moorgate

Liverpool St

London Wall

London Wall

Bishopsgate

Bishopsgate

Houndsditch

Bevis Marks

(9) **Guildhall**

Gresham St

(8)

St Paul's

Cheapside

One New Change

New Change

Bank of England

(6)

Prince's St

Threadneedle St

Cornhill

Leadenhall St

Poultry

Queen Victoria St

Bank

(5)

Mansion House

(7)

Cannon St

Lombard St

King William St

Gracechurch St

Fenchurch St

en Victoria St

Upper Thames St

Cannon St

Cannon St

King William St

Monument

Eastcheap

Great Tower St

King William St

Lower Thames St

Billingsgate

Custom House

Southwark Bridge

River Thames

CHAPTER 11

THE ARTS, ENTERTAINMENT AND HIDDEN CITY SECRETS

This final chapter is not laid out as a walk, as the attractions, museums, exhibitions and entertainments outlined are unconnected. However, in order to make it easier to locate the places, the same system of a number in square brackets (used in earlier chapters) appears beside each section and corresponds to the numbers on the chapter map.

THE BARBICAN [1]

The Barbican Centre and Estate, opened by Her Majesty The Queen in 1982, arose like a phoenix from the ashes of a totally devastated area of the City following World War II bombing. Designed by Chamberlin, Powell and Bon, its brutalist style of architecture and use of concrete remains a source of great controversy and even now continues to stir up discussion and debate among its visitors. Built on a 16-hectare (40-acre) site, the Barbican is Europe's largest multi-arts and conference centre and boasts a wonderfully spacious interior that extends over several levels. There are restaurants, shops, an art gallery, cinemas, a concert hall, conference facilities, a theatre and cafes at the site, along with a tropical plant conservatory on Level 3 (*Chapter 3).

The Barbican Centre is run by the Corporation of London and is remarkable for its breadth of arts provision. It continuously attracts the most talented pool of actors, singers, dancers, artists and musicians into its productions and exhibitions that are highly acclaimed both nationally and internationally. In addition, the

Main entrance to the Barbican Centre

Barbican Theatre

Barbican has wonderful gardens (some beside the ancient Roman wall), a central lake and external terraces where you can sit and relax.

Just across the road from the Barbican Centre in Silk Street and Milton Street is the **Guildhall School of Music and Drama**. With several theatres and a recital hall, it stages a program of musical and theatrical events throughout the year as well as voice and piano masterclasses.

Located right in the very heart of the Square Mile, a stone's throw away from one of London's major railway interchanges at Farringdon, the Barbican Centre is undoubtedly the key arts venue of the City.

MUSEUM OF LONDON [2]

If you are in the Square Mile, even for only a few hours, do try to take time to visit this very special museum that has been operating on its London Wall site since the 1970s. The present Museum of London grew from two earlier institutions, the Guildhall Museum (founded in 1826) and the London Museum (founded in 1911). When they merged in 1976, their diverse collections were combined into one, ranging from artefacts associated directly with the City of London (mainly historic, relating to livery companies, City churches and curiosities discovered in the Square Mile) to items that represented London's present as well as its past (including costumes, theatrical material and the decorative arts). In the past 40 years, the collection has continued to expand and now includes items such as archaeological and oral history archives, social and working histories as well as contemporary pieces.

The present museum is full of fascinating objects relating to London since prehistoric times and is where the story of London is explained in galleries dedicated to different periods of the city's history. The collections are exhibited on two levels: the upper, covering the period from 450,000 BC to the 1660s, and the lower, from the 1670s to the present day. Explore the museum's galleries to

Georgian Pleasure Gardens

discover the prehistoric skull of an extinct auroch (wild ox), a mammoth's tooth, the human remains of the Lant Street Teenager (a 14-year-old girl from AD100–400) and even a Roman bikini.

Visit the Medieval London gallery and see a wonderful gold and garnet brooch dating from the mid-600s as well as fashionable 14th-century leather shoes. The War, Plague & Fire gallery charts the history of the two great calamities of the 1660s – the Great Plague in 1665–6 and the Great Fire of London in 1666 – while a visit to the Roman London gallery will excite fashion devotees with its jewellery, including a jet hairpin, beads and a silver bracelet. On Level 2 you can experience the Georgian social scene in recreated **Pleasure Gardens** and be transported back to Charles Dickens' era in the **Victorian Walk**, where shops, smells and the atmosphere of 19th-century London have been meticulously reconstructed. See too the splendidly lavish **Lord Mayor's State Coach**, with its elaborate gilding, carvings and decorated panels by Giovanni Cipriani. Despite being 260 years old, the coach is still in use today and every November is driven through the streets of the City at the Lord Mayor's Parade, shortly after the inauguration of the new Lord Mayor – a wonderful example of City pageantry.

Perhaps one of the favourite galleries is **World City: 1950s-today**, as it conjures up so many memories of life in London in recent years. Here you can see a 1959 Vespa scooter, bringing back memories of the Swinging 60s London, as well as miniskirts, the fashion of Mary Quant and the Biba store plus more recent clothing and jewellery designs from Alexander McQueen and Tatty Devine.

One of the museum's newest additions is Thomas Heatherwick's London Olympic Games 2012 Cauldron. The museum has devoted an entire gallery to it; the journey of the cauldron from design to use in both the opening and closing ceremonies is beautifully described, including exciting footage of the memorable event.

With such a wonderful and diverse range of artefacts, it is not surprising that the Museum of London has become increasingly popular. Visitor numbers have doubled in the past decade, at a time when London's population has grown by over l.5 million. On account of this and the fact that the museum wants to display more of its 7 million objects, a decision has made and approved to move the museum to West Smithfield by 2021. Its new home will be the former Smithfield General, Fish and Poultry Market. These Victorian buildings will be restored and then be incorporated into the new museum. It is estimated that the project will cost about £250 million and much of the funding is to be provided by the Corporation of London and the Greater London Authority.

The museum is open daily and offers regular free gallery tours. There are two cafes, excellent cloakroom and locker facilities and an extremely well-stocked shop with a vast range of London books and other paraphernalia.

BROADGATE ICE RINK [3]

Located just moments away from Liverpool Street station, Broadgate is a major business centre within the City. Since the mid-1980s, a winter ice rink has been an annual fixture on the site. Located in Exchange Square and surrounded by food and drink stalls, it appeals as much to families as to those living in, commuting to, or merely visiting the area. Children are well catered for with penguin and seal skate aids and there is also private tuition available. The ice rink is a great wintertime favourite and certainly worth a visit if you are in town around Christmas and New Year.

BISHOPSGATE INSTITUTE [4]

The Bishopsgate Institute at 230 Bishopsgate is a well-established cultural hub offering an enormous variety of courses and events that are accessible to both City residents and visitors. Built in the late 19th century, it is set in a most impressive terracotta building designed by Charles Harrison Townsend (1851–1928). With its wide-arched entrance, intricate exterior carving and two roof turrets, it is an immediately recognisable building almost opposite Liverpool Street station. Townsend's use of Arts and Crafts, Art Nouveau, Byzantine and Romanesque architectural styles have made the Institute a handsome building and it now has Grade II*-listed status. The interior is of particular note for its magnificent Great Hall and Reference Library, panelled boardroom and mosaic floors.

The Institute runs courses during weekday mornings, afternoons and evenings as well as on weekends to allow as many people as possible to access its program. For those with limited time available, one-day courses are offered covering subjects as diverse as Iconography and Iconology as well as the Art of Meditation and Mindfulness. See www.bishopsgate.org.uk for details about events and the current program.

ESCAPE ENTERTAINMENT [5]

Located in George Yard, **EC3** [5]

This is a fabulous form of entertainment and a really unusual experience. There are several escape-room adventures and each challenges participants' problem-solving skills. The adventures have been compiled by a team of puzzle and game designers, mathematicians and psychologists, with the aim of getting people (aged 10+) to communicate and work together. Working under pressure, participants have only 60 minutes in which to work out clues, solve puzzles and find missing puzzle pieces to enable their escape from the room. The attraction is located mid-way between Cornhill and Lombard Street, and opens daily between 11.30 a.m. and 10 p.m.

BANK OF ENGLAND MUSEUM [6]

This museum is found on Bartholomew Lane, to the side of the Bank of England's main premises, and it opens weekdays from 10 a.m to 5 p.m. It is set

Bank of England Museum

Bank of England Museum, The Wind in the Willows display

in a reconstruction of the original Bank of England's Stock Office designed by Sir John Soane in the late 18th century and contains a great variety of artefacts relevant to the Bank's history. How the Bank works to protect the financial system from economic shocks and its role in today's economy are explained through its displays.

Follow the set route around the museum and you will see the original 1694 Royal Charter, discover how the bank got its nickname 'The Old Lady of Threadneedle Street', learn about the development and evolution of Bank of England notes and even have the opportunity to pick up a genuine bar of gold. Fans of Kenneth

Grahame (author of *The Wind in the Willows*) may be interested in the exhibition located in the Rotunda charting Grahame's years spent working as Secretary to the Bank. The centre of the Rotunda is also where periodic exhibitions are installed. Following the introduction of the new £10 note featuring author Jane Austen, the most recent display has been about the bank and its literary connections.

As you move towards the exit, the Modern Economy Gallery illustrates how the latest technology is used to create banknotes and in particular the new polymer notes. In this section, you can also find out about security features employed by the Bank of England to prevent forgery and counterfeit banknotes.

LONDON MITHRAEUM BLOOMBERG SPACE [**7**]

The London Mithraeum in Queen Victoria Street is an exciting exhibition space in the basement of the recently completed European headquarters of Bloomberg, the global financial and news information organisation. The company purchased the plot in 2010, knowing that the land covered a major area of Roman London alongside the now subterranean River Walbrook. It was very close to here that one of the 20th century's greatest archaeological treasures, the Roman **Temple of Mithras**, had been discovered in 1954. So extraordinary a discovery that, at the time, it attracted over 30,000 people who wanted to see the remarkable finds as they were brought up to the surface. The restored temple was later placed above ground, in front of an office block on Queen Victoria Street, where it remained until the site was cleared. At this point the temple was dismantled and put into safekeeping, so that it could be displayed once again (and then, closer to its original site) in the company's basement exhibition space.

Before construction work went ahead, excavations of the site by Museum of London Archaeology (MOLA) began. The archaeologists made some remarkable finds, throwing light on the whole of the Roman occupation of Britain between the

Roman tablet showing the first reference to the name London

1st and 5th centuries AD. Roman timber buildings and yards, clothing, documents and leather articles as well as pottery shards and fist and phallus good luck charms were discovered during their investigations. The amazing quality of their preservation is explained by the fact that they were buried in the wet mud of the River Walbrook and a lack of oxygen stopped decay – the ideal conditions for their survival.

The most significant find has been a collection of more than 400 fragments of Roman writing tablets, the earliest of any in Britain, which provide a tremendous insight into early Roman rule. The tablets were the equivalent of paper and were what the Romans used to write accounts and correspondence as well as for note taking and legal administration. To date, over 80 have been deciphered and show that Roman London was a thriving trading post inhabited by businessmen, slaves, artisans, lawmakers, soldiers and freedmen. One of the tablets dating from AD57 is the City of London's very first financial document; another containing an address – *Londinio - Mogontio* (To Mogontius in London), is the first reference to London in history.

This tablet – together with more than 700 artefacts from the excavations – is due to be displayed at Bloomberg's headquarters, along with the Temple of Mithras, when the exhibition space opens to public view in late 2017. For the latest information about opening times, go to www.bloomberg.com.

GUILDHALL ART GALLERY [8]

Sitting on the east side of Guildhall Yard, the Guildhall Art Gallery is one of the City's great gems. Only a little over 130 years old, the art gallery is home to the Corporation of London's excellent collection of paintings, sculptures and drawings that it has been amassing since 1670. The present building replaced one that had been badly damaged during 1941, and has been designed in a neo-Gothic style to complement the 14th-century Guildhall building to which it is attached.

The Guildhall Art Gallery opens every day and displays about 250 of its 4,500 artworks at any one time. It is internationally famous for its exceptional collection of Victorian art as well as its historical paintings that document London and its dramatic past. The former artworks show the chief artistic movements of the time

Guildhall Art Gallery

Guildhall Art Gallery

and include masterpieces by Frederic Leighton and the Pre-Raphaelite artists Dante Gabriel Rossetti and John Everett Millais; the latter works include scenes of everyday London as well as major paintings associated with significant London events (such as the Great Fire of London in 1666, Queen Victoria's Diamond Jubilee Service in 1897 and scenes from the Lord Mayor's Show). Of particular note is *The Defeat of the Floating Batteries at Gibraltar* by John Singleton Copley, a colossal painting extending over two floors of the main gallery. In addition temporary exhibitions are held within the gallery space and these are often free, although sometimes a small charge is made.

The Guildhall Art Gallery is also home to the **City of London Heritage Gallery**. This showcases documents that are held in trust for the nation and belong to the London Metropolitan Archives. So precious are some of these documents that members of the public have seldom seen them. The gallery aims to show London's history since 1067 through priceless documents. It is where you will find the William Charter, the charter from King John in 1215 granting the City the right to appoint its own mayor; a document entitled the Shakespeare Deed, which bears his signature (one of only six such documents in the world); and a letter from the American Congress in 1775 to the City requesting its continued backing.

Go downstairs to the basement of the Guildhall Art Gallery to see the astonishing remains of the 1st-century **Roman Amphitheatre** that are beautifully displayed in their own gallery. This gallery lies 6 m (20 ft) below ground, as for nearly 1,000

Roman Amphitheatre

years the amphitheatre was buried under successive buildings. (You can get a good idea of the size of the arena if you go outside to Guildhall Yard, where a line of black paving stones defines it.)

Historians had always expected that Roman Londinium would have its own amphitheatre but until the late 1980s nothing had come to light. Then, during the redevelopment of the Guildhall Art Gallery, workmen came across parts of the Roman wall, some as much as 1 m (3 ft) thick, and on closer investigation archaeologists realised they had stumbled upon the amphitheatre for which they had been searching. The first building was a wooden construction built about 30 years after the Roman invasion of AD43 and this was later renovated using stone in the early 2nd century, perhaps following Emperor Hadrian's visit to the city.

The amphitheatre was finally opened to public view in 2002, as it took some time for the remains to dry out. Today, on entering the gallery you walk along the entrance tunnel lined with remains of the arena's stone walls. Originally they would have stood more than 2 m (6 ft) high, supporting the wooden structure for the seating tiers above. There would have been up to 7,000 spectators sitting in the amphitheatre and enjoying savage and bloody entertainments, such as the execution of criminals, animal fights and the odd gladiatorial contest. No doubt the atmosphere was similar to that found at events in some of London's main stadiums today! There are excellent noticeboards around the gallery explaining how the amphitheatre was constructed and what it was used for, but if you want more detailed information it is probably advisable to join one of the regular tours.

Free highlight tours of the Guildhall Art Gallery, City of London Heritage Gallery and Roman Amphitheatre take place every Tuesday, Friday and Saturday, hourly between 12.15 p.m. and 3.15 p.m. There are also free audio guides available from Reception.

CITY OF LONDON POLICE MUSEUM [9]

Based within the Guildhall complex, beside Guildhall Library, this new small museum charts the history of the City's unique and dedicated police force. Since its conception in 1839, the City of London Police has been responsible for policing the Square Mile and is entirely separate from the London Metropolitan Police, coming under the auspices of the City of London Corporation.

Through its artefacts, panels and archive material, the museum tells the story of the City of London Police and the type of crimes it has dealt with over the years. A major virtual reality display relates to Catherine Eddowes, one of the victims of serial killer Jack the Ripper, while another is devoted to communications used by the force since its inception (from a mid-19th-century rattle, which was used to muster help, to present-day digital lapel radios). Other interesting artefacts include bombs manufactured by suffragettes, counterfeit money and a cabinet full of weapons seized from villains.

Despite its tiny force (about 1,100 permanent staff), it is the United Kingdom's chief police force for fraud, economic crime and cybercrime and is renowned for being at the cutting edge of technology and counter terrorism. It is easy to spot City police officers: they are the only UK force whose uniforms bear no reference to the Crown. They wear a badge containing the City of London's coat of arms on their helmet, have brass buttons on their uniform and are noted for their red and white chequered sleeve and cap bands.

CITY OF LONDON GIN DISTILLERY [10]

The City of London Gin Distillery has only been up and running since 2012 but it is already in receipt of awards for its Christopher Wren and Square Mile gins.

It is the only gin distillery in the Square Mile. Found behind a green door and located in a large basement room, the small distillery and bar can be visited on a tour. Here, you will discover how gin is distilled, find out about the botanicals added

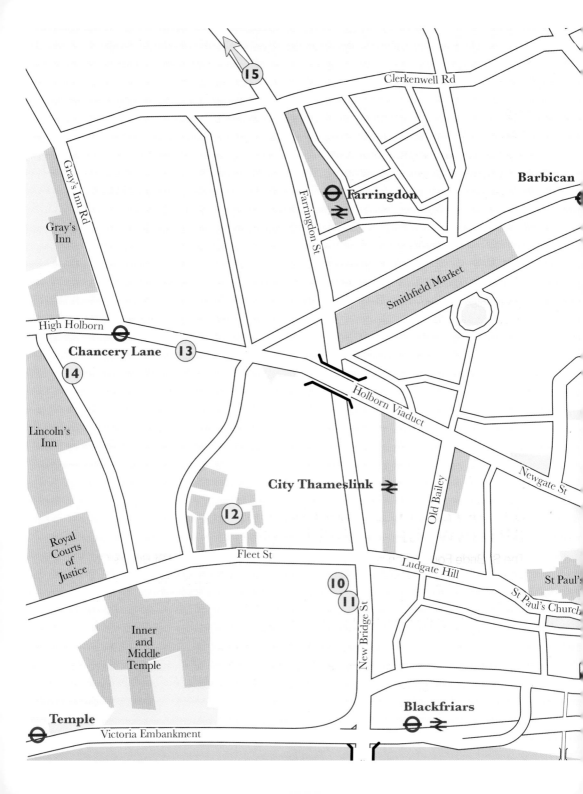

to give it its distinct taste and later have the opportunity to sample a glass of the dry gin. If you are really keen on learning about the art of gin making, you can attend a 'Gin Lab experience' where you will design your very own recipe and distil a personalised bottle of gin. Details of the tours and masterclasses can be found on www.cityoflondondistillery.com.

City of London Gin Distillery

ST BRIDE FOUNDATION AND BRIDEWELL THEATRE [11]

The St Bride Foundation is tucked away in a small street behind St Bride's Church on Fleet Street and is easy to miss if you don't know to look out for it. Today, the St Bride Foundation is a thriving arts centre offering a range of interesting and diverse 45-minute lunchtime theatrical productions. Its fringe theatre (built over the City's first swimming pool!) is an intimate space where classic and contemporary drama, opera, magic, pantomime, ballet and musicals are staged by both amateur and professional companies. The theatre also stages a number of evening productions and there is a theatre bar that sometimes hosts live music.

From its creation in 1891, the St Bride Foundation aimed to provide arts and recreational facilities for those working and living in the district and it continues on the same path today. Situated right in the middle of the print industry for much of its existence, the centre houses a comprehensive collection of print, communications and graphic design and is unique in the United Kingdom as the only library that is solely dedicated to the history of printing and allied crafts and is open to the public. It is recognised globally as a major resource and people come from far and wide to access its collections. For opening hours and current events, check online at www. sbf.org.uk.

Bridewell Theatre

DR JOHNSON'S HOUSE [12]

Set just behind Fleet Street in a warren of courts and alleys, the house is a splendid example of a 17th/18th-century London townhouse. Initially the home of a wool merchant, Samuel Johnson took up residence here between 1748 and 1759. It is where, as a fairly impoverished writer, he compiled his celebrated *Dictionary of the English Language* in the attic.

The house changed hands a number of times before it was purchased in the early 20th century by politician and newspaper magnate Cecil Harmsworth (brother of press barons Lord Rothermere and Lord Northcliffe). He restored it and then opened it to the public in 1914. Under his ownership, the house was furnished as much as possible in the style of the time when Johnson lived there.

Nowadays, a visit to the house might include an audiovisual tour of the building, where you will learn about Johnson's life and explore the townhouse with its fine panelled rooms, pine staircase and typical period furniture. There are Georgian costumes to try on and a family trail to follow. Dr Johnson's House publicises a regular program of events, including talks and lectures, concerts, evening openings, staged performances and special exhibitions.

The house is located at 17 Gough Square and you will know that you have reached your destination when you see a bronze statue of Johnson's cat, Hodge, in the courtyard. Hodge is depicted sitting on top of Johnson's dictionary, beside a pair of empty oyster shells. Part of the inscription on the plinth reads: 'a very fine cat indeed'.

Dr Johnson's House, Gough Square

GRESHAM COLLEGE [13]

The College was established at the very end of the 16th century as a bequest from the will of Sir Thomas Gresham (*Chapter 10). It has been operating ever since in the City of London, delivering free lectures.

Its initial premises were in Gresham's mansion on Bishopsgate, which served as the home and workplace of the seven Gresham Professors (including Sir Christopher Wren). Today, Gresham College is lodged in the 14th-century Barnard's Inn Hall, close to Chancery Lane station. More than 130 lectures and events are held within the Hall each year and all are free and open to the public. The lectures are remarkably wide-ranging in their content and are of the highest standard, given by Gresham Professors and visiting speakers. To gain an idea of the breadth of their provision, look online on www.gresham.ac.uk. There are 1,900 lectures that have been recorded and available to view.

Anyone can attend a lecture and it is a great privilege to do so, both for the quality of the speakers and for the venue in which they take place. Gresham College receives no government funding and is administered through the Worshipful Company of Mercers and the City of London Corporation.

LONDON SILVER VAULTS [14]

The London Silver Vaults are located at the north-western edge of the Square Mile in Chancery Lane and house the greatest retail collection of fine antique silver in the world. Sited in an attractive vaulted area protected by enormous safe doors, the specialist retailers (several of them family businesses) sell their products to both domestic and international buyers and have been doing so for more than 60 years. The London Silver Vaults is the ideal place to visit to find silver dating back to the 1500s as well as exciting contemporary works. Although the great majority of the silver is English, the retailers also stock silverware from across the globe. It

William Walter Antiques Ltd in the London Silver Vaults

is definitely the place to come to purchase silver gilt tableware, cutlery, jewellery, watches, gifts and old Sheffield Plate.

Opening hours are 9 a.m. to 5.30 p.m. from Monday to Friday and 9 a.m. to 1 p.m. on Saturday. The closest underground station is Chancery Lane (Central line).

POSTAL MUSEUM AND MAIL RAIL [15]

For 75 years the City (and the entire country) was served by an automated underground train postal system known as 'Mail Rail' that operated almost round the clock, transporting more than 4 million letters a day. The miniature mail train ran 10.4 km (6½ miles) across London, from Paddington in the west through a network of tunnels passing under the City's streets and major tourist attractions to Whitechapel in the east. The service ceased operating more than a decade ago when it became increasingly uneconomic to run and, until recently, the tunnels were unused – although several proposals had been put forward for their use, including a cycle highway and a mushroom farm!

Now, once again the tiny train is active and visitors can experience an actual journey in a replica mail train riding along the hidden subterranean tunnels. The story of Mail Rail's existence and significance is cleverly brought to life through audiovisual displays and the commentary of former company workers. At the end of the ride, you are free to wander around the Mail Rail interactive exhibition and discover firsthand how the system operated.

Mail Rail train, Postal Museum

Also part of the attraction but in another building across the road is the Postal Museum. Here you find displays charting the history of 500 years of postal life: a replica mail coach, interesting examples of early postal methods, an illuminating display about the introduction of the 'Penny Post' as well as presentations illustrating how the postal system operated during wartime (enhanced by the use of period-costumed actors).

The museum is highly accessible and attractive to visitors of every age; families in particular will appreciate its interactive facilities and children's play zone. By the exit there is a spacious cafe (with outdoor seating available) and two shops. The Postal Museum and Mail Rail is located at 15–20 Phoenix Place, just outside the Square Mile, and opens daily between 10 a.m. and 5 p.m.

And finally, for early risers …

SUNRISE YOGA

This is ideal for anyone who enjoys exercising in the clouds. Increasingly popular with Londoners – but open to anyone visiting the City – are several sky-high venues offering early-morning yoga classes. **Yoga in the Walkways** takes place 42 m (138 ft) above the Thames on the high walkways of **Tower Bridge** on Wednesdays (7.30 a.m. to 8.20 a.m.) and Saturdays (8 a.m. to 8.50 a.m.). Classes lasting an hour are held on the 36th floor of the **Walkie Talkie**, starting at 6.30 a.m. on Tuesdays to Fridays, 8 a.m. on Saturdays and 8.30 a.m. on Sundays. Alternatively, cross the Thames to **The Shard** and attend Europe's highest yoga class, at 310 m (1,017 ft) above the ground, on Saturdays at 8.30 a.m. Classes are also held on Level 24 during weekday evenings and on weekends.

TRAVEL IN LONDON

To travel around London, you will need to use one of the following: a **Visitor Oyster Card,** an **Oyster Card**, a **paper Travelcard** or a **contactless payment card.** Both VisitLondon and Transport for London (TfL) explain the systems in detail on their websites (www.visitlondon.com and www.tfl.gov.uk) but a brief summary is given below.

A **Visitor Oyster Card** for use on the Underground (tube), bus, DLR, London Overground, tram and many National Rail services in London can be purchased in advance of your visit and delivered to your home address. The card costs £3 (non-refundable) plus postage; you select how much credit to add to it. Alternatively, you can buy it on arrival at Gatwick and Stansted airports and onboard Eurostar trains to London. The card gives special offers and discounts during your stay for a number of London restaurants, attractions, shops, Thames Clippers river buses and on the Emirates Air Line cable car. There is a daily price limit on the card, so once you have reached it there is nothing more to pay.

An **Oyster Card** works in a similar way to the Visitor Oyster Card but costs £5 (refundable), is only obtained in the United Kingdom and does not include any special promotions or offers. Cards are available from Visitor Information Centres (at Heathrow and Gatwick airports; Paddington, King's Cross, Euston and Victoria mainline railway stations; and Liverpool Street and Piccadilly Circus underground stations) and at Oyster Ticket Stops in many newsagents and shops.

Contactless Payment Cards are debit, credit or prepaid cards and may be used as payment for a ticket up to a £30 limit. There is no need to use a PIN or a signature. If your contactless card has been issued outside the United Kingdom, you should first check if your bank charges transaction fees for usage on the London transport system.

Paper Travelcards, like Oyster Cards, can be used on the underground, bus, DLR, London Overground, tram and many National Rail services in London. They will cover certain zones (London is divided into Zones 1–9) and last for one day only. As with a Visitor Oyster Card, you will obtain discounts on various riverboat services and also on the Emirates Air Line cable car. A seven-day Travelcard is also available but can only be loaded onto an Oyster Card.

Note:

- When using Oyster Cards and Contactless Payment Cards, you **must** touch the yellow card reader at the gates at the start and end of your journey or you could get charged a penalty fare.
- On **buses and trams,** you only need to touch the yellow card reader at the **start** of your journey.

Only Oyster Cards **or** Contactless Payment Cards can be used on buses. No cash is accepted.

Credit can be added to your Oyster Card or Visitor Oyster Card at the touchscreen ticket machines in Underground, London Overground, DLR and some National Rail stations as well as at Oyster Ticket Stops, from Visitor and Travel Information Centres and at Emirates Air Line terminals.

Transport for London (TfL) buses

These are mainly the classic double-decker red buses for which London is renowned and they are good to use around the centre of town. Information about timetables and routes is available on the TfL website but it may be useful to know that bus numbers 11 and 15 run past most of the tourist hotspots:

11: From Liverpool Street via the City to Victoria, Sloane Square, King's Road to Fulham Broadway

15: From Trafalgar Square to Blackwall via Tower Hill and Aldgate.

Private tourist buses

There are several hop-on/hop-off services offering live commentary in English as well as recorded information in a number of other languages. With tickets ranging in price from £25 to £30 per day, this can be a good way to see many of the sights if you are only in London for a brief visit.

Black taxi cabs and minicab services

You will see black cabs everywhere (unless it is raining hard!) and fares are determined by the length of the journey and time of day. Other cab services include Uber, Addison Lee and local minicab hire, the details of which can be found online.

Santander Cycles

This is certainly a cheap way to get round London. You can hire a Santander Cycle for as little as £2, which is ideal for short trips. You just need to take a credit or debit card to the docking terminal and follow the instructions on the screen. The first 30 minutes of each journey is free and longer journeys cost £2 for each extra 30 minutes. Refer to the TfL website (www.tfl.gov.uk) for more detailed information about the self-service bicycle hire scheme.

GLOSSARY

Historical periods

Roman	AD43–410
Anglo-Saxon	410–1066
Norman	1066–1154
Plantagenet	1154–1399
Lancastrian	1399–1471
House of York	1460–1485
Tudor	1485–1603
Stuart	1603–1714
Georgian	1714–1837
Victorian	1837–1901
Edwardian	1901–1910

Art and architectural terms

Adamesque	The neoclassical architectural style attributed to the three Adam brothers – John, Robert and James – during the latter part of the 18th century. With reference to ancient civilisations, their style integrated both architecture and interiors, including the furniture, furnishings, walls and ceilings.
Art Deco	An architectural and decorative style of the 1920s and 1930s that used vibrant colours and patterns.

Art Nouveau	A popular style between 1890 and 1910, which is often characterised by its curves and swirling decoration.
Arts and Crafts	This movement gathered momentum in the late 19th/early 20th century, in response to the mass-produced goods of the Industrial Revolution. It promoted a return to skilled quality craftsmanship, using simple designs and local materials.
Baroque	A flamboyant and monumental architectural style in fashion from 1600 to 1750.
Brutalism	A term used in the mid-20th century to describe Le Corbusier's architecture. It features rough or raw concrete, often in large forms.
Edwardian	Covers the styles mainly in use during the reign of King Edward VII (r.1901–1910), such as Gothic Revival, neo-Georgian and Baroque Revival.
Georgian	The style of art and architecture between 1714 and 1830, during the reigns of George I, II, III and IV, when classical proportions were introduced into all types of buildings.
Gothic	Refers to the style of the Middle Ages, which is renowned for its pointed arches, rib vaulting and large windows. Covers the period from around 1180 to 1520 and is divided into Early English Gothic, Decorated and Perpendicular styles.
High Tech	This style emerged in the 1970s, when designers selected lightweight building materials. It is

	characterised by the external exposure of mechanical services.
Italianate	This style of architecture was most prevalent in the early to mid-19th century. It is used in secular buildings and based on palatial homes in Renaissance Italy.
Modernism	This art and architectural style of the 20th century discarded adornment and used modern materials in a minimalist fashion. It is typified by the use of reinforced concrete, iron, steel, metal and glass.
Palladian	Properly formulated, elegant and classical architecture introduced into England from the early 17th century.
Pre-Raphaelite Brotherhood	A group of mid-19th-century British painters who, in opposition to the Royal Academy's historical art teaching of the period, wanted to reintroduce the style and essence of Italian artists from before the time of Raphael.
Postmodernism	A late 20th century movement that departed from functional, conventional architecture. It merged art and functionality – creating an 'anything goes' culture – and incorporated the unusual use of colour and materials, historical elements and decoration.

WEB ADDRESSES BY CHAPTER

Chapter 1

Museum of London Archaeology	www.mola.org.uk
Tower Bridge	www.towerbridge.org.uk
Tower of London	www.hrp.org.uk

Chapter 2

Mansion House	www.cityoflondon.gov.uk
The Royal Exchange	www.theroyalexchange.co.uk
Bank of England	www.bankofengland.co.uk
Leadenhall Market	www.cityoflondon.gov.uk
Lloyd's of London	www.lloyds.com
Drapers' Company	www.thedrapers.co.uk
Guildhall	www.cityoflondon.gov.uk
London Stock Exchange	www.londonstockexchange.com

Chapter 3

Middle Temple	www.middletemple.org.uk
Inner Temple	www.innertemple.org.uk
City Information Centre	www.cityoflondon.gov.uk

Chapter 4

One New Change	www.onenewchange.com
Bloomberg Place	www.bloomberg.com
Cannon Place	www.cannonplace.co.uk
The Walbrook	www.fosterandpartners.com
Riverbank House	www.davidwalkerarchitects.com
The Monument	www.themonument.org.uk
20 Fenchurch Street	www.skygarden.london

Canary Wharf	www.group.canarywharf.com
Lloyd's of London	www.lloyds.com
Willis Building	www.willis.com
The Scalpel	www.thescalpelec3.co.uk
Cheesegrater	www.theleadenhallbuilding.com
The Trellis	www.ericparryarchitects.co.uk
The Gherkin	www.thegherkinlondon.com
60–70 St Mary Axe	www.foggo.com
Tower 42	www.tower42.com
The Heron Tower	www.herontower.com
Broadgate	www.broadgate.co.uk

Chapter 5

City Events	www.london-city-churches.org.uk
St Paul's Cathedral	www.stpauls.co.uk
St Mary-le-Bow	www.stmarylebow.co.uk
St Mary Aldermary	www.stratmanrocker.uk
	www.stmaryaldermary.co.uk
St Stephen Walbrook	www.ststephenwalbrook.net
St Michael's Cornhill	www.st-michaels.org.uk
St Helen's Bishopsgate	www.st-helens.org.uk
Bevis Marks Synagogue	www.sephardi.org.uk
St Ethelburga's	www.stethelburgas.org
St Lawrence Jewry	www.stlawrencejewry.org.uk

Chapter 6

College of Arms	www.college-of-arms.gov.uk
St Paul's Cathedral	www.stpauls.co.uk
St Bartholomew's Hospital	www.bartshealth.nhs.uk
St Bartholomew the Great	www.greatstbarts.com

Smithfield Market	www.smithfieldmarket.com
Postman's Park	www.postmanspark.org.uk
Goldsmiths' Company	www.thegoldsmiths.co.uk
The Guildhall	www.guildhall.cityoflondon.gov.uk
Broadgate	www.broadgate.co.uk
Tower of London	www.hrp.org.uk
Tower Bridge Exhibition	www.towerbridge.org.uk
Jamaica Wine House	www.jamaicawinehouse.co.uk

Chapter 7

Royal Courts of Justice	www.justice.gov.uk
Temple Bar	www.cityoflondon.gov.uk
St Dunstan-in-the-West	www.stdunstaninthewest.org
Middle Temple	www.middletemple.org.uk
Inner Temple	www.innertemple.org.uk
Temple Church	www.templechurch.com
College of Arms	www.college-of-arms.gov.uk
St Paul's Cathedral	www.stpauls.co.uk
The Old Bailey	www.old-bailey.com/visiting-the-old-bailey

Chapter 8

Searcy's	www.searcysatthegherkin.co.uk
One New Change	www.onenewchange.com
Madison	www.madisonlondon.net
Coq d'Argent	www.coqdargent.co.uk
The Ned Hotel	www.thened.com
Angler Restaurant	www.anglerrestaurant.com
Shoryu Ramen	www.shoryuramen.com
Yauatcha City	www.yauatcha.com
Jamies Wine Bar	www.jamies.london

Barbecoa	www.barbecoa.com
La Chapelle	www.galvinrestaurants.com
Kenza	www.kenza-restaurant.com
Cinnamon Kitchen	www.cinnamon-kitchen.com
The Bull and the Hide	www.thebullandthehide.com
Hawksmoor Guildhall	www.thehawksmoor.com
Sauterelle	www.royalexchange-grandcafe.co.uk
Sweetings Restaurant	www.sweetingsrestaurant.co.uk
Club Gascon	www.clubgascon.com
Vanilla Black	www.vanillablack.co.uk
Simpson's Tavern	www.simpsonstavern.co.uk
Duck and Waffle	www.duckandwaffle.com
Sushi Samba	www.sushisamba.com
Vertigo 42	www.vertigo42.co.uk
City Social	www.citysociallondon.com
Fenchurch Restaurant, Darwin Brasserie	www.skygarden.london
Middle Temple Hall dining	www.events@middletemple.org.uk
Café Below	www.cafebelow.co.uk
The Viaduct Tavern	www.viaducttavern.co.uk
The Blackfriar	www.nicholsonspubs.co.uk
The Punch Tavern	www.punchtavern.com
Ye Olde Cock Tavern	www.greeneking-pubs.co.uk
The Old Bank of England	www.oldbankofengland.co.uk
The Old Bell Tavern	www.nicholsonspubs.co.uk
El Vino	www.elvino.co.uk
The Knights Templar	www.jdwetherspoon.com
The Bishop's Finger	www.thebishopsfinger.co.uk
Butchers Hook & Cleaver	www.butchershookandcleaver.co.uk
The Hope	www.thehopesmithfield.co.uk

Rising Sun	www.risingsunbarbican.co.uk
Fox & Anchor	www.foxandanchor.com
Williamson's Tavern	www.nicholsonspubs.co.uk
Jamaica Wine House	www.jamaicawinehouse.co.uk
The Counting House	www.the-counting-house.com
The Crosse Keys	www.jdwetherspoon.com
The Lamb Tavern	www.lambtavernleadenhall.com
The Hoop and Grapes	www.nicholsonspubs.co.uk
Dirty Dicks	www.dirtydicks.co.uk
Hamilton Hall	www.jdwetherspoon.com
The Hung Drawn and Quartered	www.hung-drawn-and-quartered.co.uk
Swingers	www.swingersldn.com
Bounce	www.bouncepingpong.com
Flight Club	www.flightclubdarts.com
Whistle Punks	www.whistlepunks.com
London Shuffle Club	www.london.shuffle.com
Junkyard Golf Club	www.junkyardgolfclub.co.uk
The Mayor of Scaredy Cat Town	www.themayorofscaredycattown.com
The Bootlegger	www.thebootlegger.co.uk
Proud Cabaret City	www.proudcabaretcity.com

Chapter 9

Middle Temple Hall	www.middletemple.org.uk
Temple Church	www.templechurch.com
St Dunstan-in-the-West	www.stdunstaninthewest.org
St Bride's Church	www.stbrides.com
St Sepulchre Without Newgate Church	www.stsepulchres.org
St Bartholomew the Great	www.greatstbarts.com
All Hallows by the Tower	www.allhallowsbythetower.org.uk
Tower of London	www.hrp.org.uk

Chapter 10

John Wesley	www.wesleysheritage.org.uk
Temple Bar Gate	www.cityoflondon.gov.uk
	www.stpauls.co.uk
Paternoster Square	www.paternostersquare.info
Royal Exchange	www.theroyalexchange.co.uk
St Olave Hart Street	www.sanctuaryinthecity.net
Sir John Cass	www.sirjohncassfoundation.com

Chapter 11

The Barbican	www.barbican.org.uk
Guildhall School of Music and Drama	www.gsmd.ac.uk
Museum of London	www.museumoflondon.org.uk
Broadgate (Ice Rink)	www.broadgate.co.uk
Bishopsgate Institute	www.bishopsgate.org.uk
Escape Hunt	www.escapehunt.com
Bank of England Museum	www.bankofengland.co.uk
London Mithraeum	www.bloomberg.com
Guildhall Art Gallery and Amphitheatre	www.cityoflondon.gov.uk
City of London Police Museum	www.cityoflondon.police.uk
City of London Gin Distillery	www.cityoflondondistillery.com
St Bride Foundation and Bridewell Theatre	www.sbf.org.uk
Dr Johnson's House	www.drjohnsonshouse.org
Gresham College	www.gresham.ac.uk
Silver Vaults	www.silvervaultslondon.com
Postal Museum	www.postalmuseum.org

INDEX

First published in 2018 by New Holland Publishers
London • Sydney • Auckland

131–151 Great Titchfield Street, London WIW 5BB, United Kingdom
1/66 Gibbes Street, Chatswood, NSW 2067, Australia
5/39 Woodside Ave, Northcote, Auckland 0627, New Zealand

newhollandpublishers.com

A record of this book is held at the British Library and the National Library of Australia.

ISBN 9781742579801

Group Managing Director: Fiona Schultz
Publisher: Alan Whiticker
Project Editor: Danielle Viera
Designer: Andrew Davies
Production Director: James Mills-Hicks
Printer: Times Offset (M) Sdn Bhd, Malaysia

10 9 8 7 6 5 4 3 2 1

Keep up with New Holland Publishers on Facebook
facebook.com/NewHollandPublishers

IMAGE CREDITS

All photographs in this book are © A McMurdo except:

p5 Beefeaters © Historic Royal Palaces; p63 Lord Mayor's Show © Clive Totman; p69 Temple
Gardens © The Honourable Society of the Middle Temple; p101 Walkie Talkie © Rhubarb;
p119 Inside St Paul's Cathedral © Graham Lacdao; p171 Middle Temple & p173 Middle Temple
Hall © The Honourable Society of the Middle Temple; p188 Grand Café © The Royal Exchange;
p190 Duck and Waffle © Duck & Waffle; p191 Sky Garden © Rhubarb; p200 View of the Tower
42 © James Byrne Photography; p262 Barbican Centre & Barbican Theatre © Max Colson;
p264 Georgian Pleasure Gardens © Museum of London; p270 Roman tablet © Andy Chopping/
MOLA; p282 Mail Rail Train © The Postal Museum/Miles Willis.